# Praise for SUCCESS BOUND

*"This is a great book. I've read nearly every book about success and let me tell you, that reading this book is a must. No one will be able to break free of mediocrity and get on the road to success unless they have first learned how to manage their failures. The 21 strategies in this book are indeed proven; they have worked in my life – they can work in yours too."*

> **– Peter Lowe**, Success Strategist; Host and Editor, "Peter Lowe's Success Talk"; and Founder of the internationally acclaimed "Peter Lowe Success Seminars" (www.PeterLowe.com)

*"This is a wonderful book. It is full of tremendous insights, practical methods and techniques, and proven strategies that you can use as springboards to greater success in every part of your life."*

> **– Brian Tracy,** author of "The 100 Absolutely Unbreakable Laws of Business Success" and "Maximum Achievement" (www.BrianTracy.com)

*"If you're ready to be permanently success bound, read this book!"*

> **– Mark Victor Hansen**, Co-creator, #1 *New York Times* best-selling series *Chicken Soup for the Soul*® (www.MarkVictorHansen.com)

*"Every once in a while, someone comes along who can lead the leaders. Randy Gilbert has captured the essence of appropriating an abundant life in SUCCESS BOUND. I highly recommend everyone read it, because truly great leaders learn how to embrace their failures and turn them into the fuel that propels them ever further toward their goals."*

> **– John C. Maxwell**, author of, "Failing Forward – Turning Mistakes into Stepping Stones for Success," "21 Irrefutable Laws of Leadership – Follow Them and People Will Follow You," and "The Winning Attitude – Your Pathway To Personal Success" (www.INJOY.com)

*"This is an amazing book! I can think of 101 reasons why you should read SUCCESS BOUND. Let me start you out with the most important – the strategies Randy Gilbert outlines will bring you the success you deserve. Read it, and you will discover the other 100 reasons for yourself."*
  **– Raleigh Pinskey**, author of "101 Ways to Promote Yourself"
  (www.PromoteYourself.com)

*"I've known Randy since he was a young Lieutenant in the Coast Guard. This book wonderfully reflects his honest, highly motivated, straightforward and always positive self. It is obvious that his caring about others and his sincere desire for them to succeed has brought about his own success. If you want to be success bound, read Randy's book, and then get busy helping others find this wisdom too."*
  **– Vice Admiral James C. Card, USCG (ret.)**, 21st Vice
  Commandant of the U.S. Coast Guard

*"I have said: if you can't manage your failures, you'll never get an opportunity to see how you do handling success. In SUCCESS BOUND, Randy Gilbert has assembled a robust collection of ideas, stories and simple, practical suggestions for converting adversity, frustration, and failure into positives."*
  **– Dan S. Kennedy**, CEO, the Psycho-Cybernetics Foundation
  (www.psycho-cybernetics.com), author, "NO RULES: 21 Lies &
  Myths About Success" (www.DanKennedy.com)

*"In his wonderfully written book, SUCCESS BOUND author Randy Gilbert reveals so many insights about failure that readers will either learn to embrace it or avoid it completely. I give a high five to Randy for combining practical wisdom with spiritual enlightenment."*
  **– Jay Conrad Levinson**, author, "Guerrilla Marketing" series of
  books (www.GMarketing.com)

*"Randy Gilbert teaches that failure is but a friend in disguise. SUCCESS BOUND is an important book for all overcomers."*
  **– Laurie Beth Jones**, author of "Jesus, CEO", "The Path", and
  "Jesus, Inc." (www.JesusCEO.com)

*"Failure is not a destination but an opportunity. It is a question of attitude and what you learn from each setback. Randy Gilbert reveals how to use obstacles to succeed. This is one of the most upbeat, inspirational, can-do, will-do books I have ever read."*
  – **Dan Poynter**, author of "The Self-Publishing Manual"
  (www.ParaPublishing.com)

*"Randy Gilbert has written a great book that takes a new look at success and what it takes to get there. It's a gem! Give this book to anyone who's failing and get them to read it once a week. Check back with them in five years and you'll probably find them to be a roaring success."*
  – **Roger Dawson**, author of "Secrets of Power Negotiating"
  (www.RDawson.com)

*"Once in a while I discover a GREAT new book. Believe me, Randy has all of the greatness bells pealing with SUCCESS BOUND! It reminds me of Steve Allen's "Meeting of the Minds" TV show in which characters from different historical eras meet and talk together. Every page introduces "Friends of the Mind" who will lift up your spirit, fire up your resolve, and ignite the spirit that slumbers within your heart. I need 10 more thumbs to give you enough thumbs up!*

*My suggestion: Purchase a whole stack of SUCCESS BOUND books with its 21 strategies! Then you won't have to waste time shopping when you need a TREASURE GIFT for your friends and family. Tears will come to your eyes as they did to mine, as you recognize the stream of intelligence as you hear the voices in this book helping you, encouraging you, awakening you, and reminding you."*
  – **Dottie Walters**, International Speaker, (www.Walters-Intl.com)
  Author of "Speak & Grow Rich"
  Publisher/Editor: "SHARING IDEAS" Speaker magazine, 23rd year
  President, Walters International Speakers Bureau
  Publisher International Directory of Speakers Bureaus
  Founder: Association of Speaker Bureau Owners

*"So many books seem to create more questions in my mind than they do to provide solutions and direction. SUCCESS BOUND clearly provides specific answers and gives clear directions to anyone who wants true success and yet has been frustrated by failure. Next to the Bible, it could be the most "freeing" book a person might read. I would encourage anyone who doesn't feel they've attained the level of success God desires for them to read this book. More importantly, anyone who doesn't understand or believe my last sentence MUST read SUCCESS BOUND, especially the last chapter."*

> – **Al Walker**, President of Al Walker & Associates, Inc.; a firm dedicated to helping businesses and individuals become more productive. (www.AlWalker.com)

*"Train your brain to go for and get success by following the proven strategies so nicely laid out in this cool book. Excellent!"*

> – **Joe Vitale**, author, "There's A Customer Born Every Minute" and many other books. (www.MrFire.com)

*"We all fear change at some level. This book will help you to break through those fears and create the success you deserve."*

> – **Debbie Allen**, author of "Confessions of Shameless Self Promoters" (www.ConfessionsofShamelessSelfPromoters.com)

Author's note: If after reading this book you would like to provide a testimonial to be listed in future revisions, or on the book's web site (with an active link to your web site), then please send it to: Randy@DrProactive.com

# SUCCESS BOUND

## *Breaking Free of Mediocrity*

# Randy Gilbert

First Edition

**Bargain Publishers Company, Inc.,
Mt. Jackson, Virginia**

## SUCCESS BOUND – Breaking Free of Mediocrity

Published by Bargain Publishers Co., Inc., Mt. Jackson, Virginia

Printed in the United States of America

This book is available in:

| | | | |
|---|---|---|---|
| E-book format: | ISBN | 0-9707517-2-9 |
| Paperback: | ISBN | 0-9707517-0-2 |
| Hardcover: | ISBN | 0-9707517-1-0 |

The e-book and numerous related articles and free reports can be found on the internet at: http://www.Success–Bound.com.

The cover art is from an oil painting called, *West Maui Rainbow*, by Georgiana Chan. Used by permission.

All Biblical references are paraphrased; however, they have been learned and memorized from several well-known and trusted translations.

Library of Congress Cataloging-in-Publication Number 2001116243

# TABLE OF CONTENTS

# DEDICATION

To the men and women of the United States Coast Guard, who serve so faithfully and unselfishly to protect the environment and the lives of the people who recreate and make their living on or near the water, and

More specifically, to Jeffrey Georges, a member of the USCG Academy graduating class of 1978, whose last wish prior to his untimely death was for his classmates to write something so that his young children might be able to know us, even though their Daddy would not be able to introduce us to them; thus

It is to Jeff and his family that I dedicate this book. May the Georges family always be as SUCCESS BOUND as Jeff had been; and still is, though in a different place. Although your lives may be challenged by struggles, adversity, and even failures, it is my sincere wish that you will be filled with wisdom, abundance, and lots of love. I hope and pray that this book will assist you in all of your adventures in life.

# ABOUT THE AUTHOR

**Randy "Dr. Proactive" Gilbert** is an authority on the philosophy of proactive thinking, of which he now writes, speaks, and consults. He teaches how to proactively optimize safety, quality and business processes in order to ensure maximum success and achievement. In his personal quest for excellence he has learned that managing ones failures is a key to personal success and abundance. As Dr. Proactive, he helps people and organizations rid themselves of problems as they plan for a successful future. He is a delightful and entertaining speaker who knows how to motivate an audience to believe and practice proactive thinking.

Randy earned a Bachelors degree from the U.S. Coast Guard Academy and a Masters degree from the University of Michigan. He served in the Coast Guard for 22 years, of which 16 were in maritime safety. He and his wife Cathy have three grown children who were home-schooled all the way up through high school. Randy and Cathy now live in the beautiful Shenandoah Valley in the State of Virginia. You can find out more about him at: http://www.RandyGilbert.com

# SUPPORT FOR THE COAST GUARD FOUNDATION

Randy Gilbert is donating a portion of the proceeds from the sale of the paperback and hardcover versions of this book to the Coast Guard Foundation. The Coast Guard Foundation helps to provide support for the U.S. Coast Guard Academy as well as all of the Coast Guard programs. If you want to learn more about the Coast Guard Foundation visit: http://www.cgfdn.org

# FOREWORD

Dear Reader of SUCCESS BOUND,

Is saying "I've become a successful failure" an oxymoron? I don't think so. For the longest time I felt my life was in limbo. Real success, the kind that comes with abundant life and joy, eluded me. I felt I was meant to do more, but I feared failure. I had a case of 'FAILURE-itis !'

Like most people I took the wait-and-see approach to failures and invariably followed a life of just getting by – a life of mediocrity. Because of my fear of failure, I limited myself to what came along. But then I discovered the 21 strategies outlined in this book. By using them I learned how to manage my failures and have broken free of mediocrity. I feel confident in saying that instead of being bound by failure, I am now SUCCESS BOUND. I pass these 21 strategies on to you so you can benefit by them. I have wonderfully cured myself of FAILURE-itis – and you can too!

This book is about how you can succeed by managing your failures and set yourself free to pursue your dreams. It is not a guide about how to enjoy failures; rather, it contains the wisdom needed for managing the adversities, defeats, shortcomings, mistakes, problems, struggles, "bad hair days," unfortunate circumstances, etc. that will inevitably visit you in life. It is a fresh new approach to personal achievement that will empower you to give it all you've got.

> *How you deal with failure determines whether or not you ever get the opportunity to deal with success.*
> Dan Kennedy

There are many books about how to succeed in a myriad of ways. Failure is a subject that is always mentioned; but never fully explained! Some of them go so far as to say that you cannot succeed unless you first learn how to fail; but then they leave you hanging. This book fills in all of those blank pages, by fully addressing strategies of how to manage failure, so that your success will be all but guaranteed.

You will learn to proactively approach failures in such a way as to take advantage of them. Failures will become your opportunities for success and abundance, rather than defeat and deprivation. Einstein said, "Every problem holds the seeds of an equal or greater opportunity." However, these are problem seeds that must be nurtured with care. If you follow the strategies outlined in this book, opportunities will grow and failures will be transformed into wealth, wisdom, and whatever else you desire in life.

My best wishes to you on your own SUCCESS BOUND journey,

*Randy Gilbert*
*(http://www.RandyGilbert.com)*

# ACKNOWLEDGEMENTS

My foremost appreciation goes to my wife Cathy, who has encouraged me and has been a true helpmate throughout my career. I especially appreciate her confidence in me – knowing that the waters of writing and speaking are more turbulent than business and far less certain than serving in the Coast Guard. She has overlooked my faults and forgiven my failures. Best of all, she has shared her wisdom and love with me. She is the best.

> *If we all did the things we are capable of doing, we would literally astound ourselves.*
> Thomas Edison

My children, Michelle, Timothy, and Deborah, have been instrumental in helping me to be successful, taking on the job of editors of my work, even when they were very young. Although Cathy and I tutored them at home (i.e. home-schooled them), I believe they have taught me more than I've taught them. Each of them has lived up to Leonardo da Vinci's saying, "The student at some point should exceed the master." I look forward to reading their books someday.

Deborah was especially helpful in launching this book and spent much of her sophomore summer researching and editing for me. When it comes to writing I have two strikes against me: I grew up speaking Hawaii's Pidgin English as my first language, and I am an engineer and tend to think and write like one. Deborah painstakingly worked out the problems and was an immense help when it came to organizing and presenting each strategy. However, if there remain any faults with spelling, grammar, or substance, they are mine. If there is praise to be given for any parts of the book that are well written, it all goes to Deborah.

Michelle, who is now a professional film artist and animator, gave me the beautiful sketches that are included for each of the parts. They say "a picture is worth a thousand words," but in this case I believe it's more like 10 thousand. Thank you Michelle.

I also deeply appreciate all of my mentors, friends and co-workers who have spent so much of their time helping me in ways that I can only begin to recognize. I am truly grateful to so many that have freely shared their wisdom. I count among my friends all of the wonderful people, many of whom are quoted in this book, who have taken the time to write down their experiences, thoughts, insights, and wisdom. Most of them I have never met and I look forward to someday meeting them. Some of them have passed on and I will have to wait until we meet in glory. Until then, I am SUCCESS BOUND because of their faithful service to humanity. It is my hope that I will be able to be as faithful and wise a servant as they have been.

I particularly want to thank Joe Vitale, who wrote a wonderful little book, *Turbocharge Your Writing*, which laid out a clear and simple formula for success in writing that helped me figure out how to get this book past the dream stage. Finally, to my good friends, Karen McIver, Vic Primeaux, and Jack Spencer, who helped sharpen the focus and spiritual insight of this book so all readers would benefit.

# INTRODUCTION

Too often people are taught to focus on the need to succeed at everything they do, when in actuality they should strive to act in such a way that they can allow failure to happen more often. At first glance, that statement seems to be an absurdity. However, if you view it through the *Law of Probability*, you will see that as you increase your rate of trial-and-error, you increase your chances of success. Your faults and failings exist for a purpose – to help you succeed.

Picture the following. You're standing in a basketball court at the free-throw line, holding a basketball and thinking about whether or not you will be successful in making a basket. One thing is for certain, no matter what your skill level, if you don't toss the ball up toward the basket, there is zero chance of successfully making a basket. The goal is making a basket. If you don't take a chance you are missing all opportunities for achieving success.

Now let's say that you aren't a very good basketball player (like me), but you want to succeed, so you make the effort to try. Even if you have never thrown a ball in your life, you will, by the *Law of Probability*, eventually make a basket. If you keep at it long enough – if you adopt the "learn and do" attitude – you <u>will</u> get better and better.

> *There are certain things in which mediocrity is not to be endured, such as poetry, music, painting, and public speaking.*
>
> Bruyere

How many times do you have to fail at something in order to succeed? I believe it is different for each person. Thomas Edison had to fail 10,000 times at making a light bulb that would last for more than a few moments. He had a "learn and do" attitude. He turned each failed experiment into a successful way <u>not</u> to invent the light bulb. Since he was probably smarter than you, how many times might you have to fail at some big achievement before reaching success?

If you had to fail 100 times before becoming a success and you only failed once a year, you might not live long enough to become a success. Do you see the picture? If you don't allow yourself to fail or realize when you fail on a regular and more frequent basis, then you might not ever become a success in this lifetime. That is why you must be a "successful failure."

Perhaps you're thinking that not everyone can be a Thomas Edison and make such a monumental discovery as the light bulb. You are right of course, but only because not everyone discovers what their major purpose in life is and then learns to manage their failures in a systematic way until they reach their goals.

No one ever makes 10 out of 10 baskets consistently, not even Michael Jordan. Even 5 out of 10 is an excellent player. The famous baseball player Babe Ruth is known for the record number 851 home runs that he hit in his career. But few people know what it takes to attain a record like that. It took Babe Ruth a record number of strikeouts. He failed 1,330 times. But did he complain? No way!

You will improve the fastest if you are coached. Let this book speak to you as a coach would. When it comes to your major purpose in life, you only need to succeed consistently, not every time. It's like being a professional ball player. To me, one major success is worth all of the 99 failures I have to put up with along the way.

*Notice the difference between what happens when a man says to himself, I have failed three times, and what happens when he says, I am a failure.*
    S.I. Hayakawa

No one ever knows all there is to know about a subject, so it would be absurd for you to wait for that fictitious day of perfection before you applied yourself. Your life would remain unfulfilling and bound to mediocrity. Therefore, you must bravely reach out for your purposes in life, knowing that you are going to fail on a routine basis. Since you know you are going to fail, wouldn't it be in your best interest to learn how to manage your failures so that you can become successful more quickly and easily?

Tying yourself to mediocrity and not striking out in pursuit of your passion or major purpose in life is the worst failure of all. One of my friends used to say, "The only fishermen that don't catch fish are those who don't put their hooks in the water." You are not perfect; NOBODY IS! We are all in the same boat in that regard. Everyone needs the help of others to overcome their shortcomings. This book is my assistance to you. You will need other people to help you along the way. I recommend that you find others to help you who also regularly practice managing their failures. You can usually tell who they are because they have a winning attitude and a positive approach to life. I call them proactive thinkers.

Everyone has a fear of failure to some extent. Some people are more averse to failures and will try harder to stay safely within a comfort zone. This fear of failure causes stagnation in your growth and inhibits change, even if it is for your own good and happiness. I have found that by learning how to manage my failures in a proactive way, I am less afraid to fail. I can continually stretch my comfort zone and achieve more of what I understand to be my purpose in life. Managing my failures has given me fulfillment, happiness and peace of mind – Who could ask for anything more?

It is best to have a healthy approach to "troubleshooting" failures. Because some people get into a real panic when something goes wrong, they can't even notice the most obvious things. My son Tim helps a lot of people with troubleshooting computer problems, and he was recently telling us of a frantic person whose computer stopped working. Tim started down his list of most probable faults and asked the person to check the cord in the back. The person responded saying he couldn't see it very well. When Tim asked why, the upset person responded, "because the electricity is out and only the emergency light is on."

> *Success always lies on the far side of failure.*
> Thomas Watson

Of course we all had a good laugh, but I couldn't help feeling sorry for that person who probably approached other problems in his life with the same level of panic. If you have a fear of failure, this book is for you.  Even if you are not afraid of troubleshooting things when they go wrong, you will find this book helpful because it will assist you with solving problems proactively.

One of the wonderful things about life is that everyone can be "an expert" at their major purpose in life.  Napoleon Hill said that, "Whatever your mind can conceive and believe, it can achieve." Part of the believing process is learning and gathering resources so that you can eventually get very good at what you do.  Brian Tracy became one of America's most notable business achievement consultants because he discovered, "You can learn anything you need to learn in order to achieve any goal you set for yourself."

Throughout this book you will be reminded of Napoleon Hill's philosophy, "every adversity brings with it the seed of an equal advantage."  Keeping a positive attitude and looking for the advantage is not easy, especially immediately after suffering a setback.  However, you will find it to be a lot easier if you acquire the right tools to master failure now, rather than waiting until after a really difficult blow has knocked you down or you feel like you've received a knockout punch.

In this book I will teach you the 21 proven strategies for managing failures that I have learned.  I believe they are essential to your success, and I assure you that if you learn and practice them you will be more successful in everything you do.  I explain each one in turn, using examples and outlining practical steps for you to take so that you will know how to fail in the right way – the way that keeps you SUCCESS BOUND.

I feel so strongly that these strategies will literally guarantee your happiness and success in life that I will give you an unconditional guarantee on the book.  If you are not happier and more successful within 12 months of reading and following these strategies, then return the book and receipt, along with a note explaining your circumstances, and I will provide a full refund back to you.

# *Part I*

# *Rainbows After The Rain*

*Let's see if I have this right. To make a rainbow cake I need 1 cup of adversity, 2 tablespoons of optimism, 1/4 teaspoon of failure, and 2 cups of faith. Yes sir, this is going to be a beauty!*

**Foreword to Part I**

I was born in Rochester NY, but my family moved to Hawaii when I was very young.  In Hawaii, I experienced spectacular rainbows. I spent many years living in an area that is now the "Kapalua Resort," just west of Lahaina on the island of Maui.  For most of the year, Kapalua has idyllic weather, like the legendary Camelot, where it rained a little in the morning and a little in the evening, but the rest of the day was sunny and beautiful.

I say that I experienced those Hawaiian rainbows intentionally, because on Maui you don't just see them; those rainbows are so beautiful, and have such vivid colors, that you can actually feel them.  They would actually give me goose bumps all over.  But, even with Hawaiian rainbows you need to have the rain in order to have a rainbow.

To me, the rain represents failures.  Failures are those things in our lives that we need even though they make us uncomfortable.  We may not always realize it, but we need to experience the things that make us struggle, that deepen our character, and that show us our mistakes and shortcomings.

Those moments of adversity are necessary in order to experience spectacular successes.  If you want more rainbows in your life, then you must have the right attitude about the rain.  The rain makes the flowers come alive; it cleans the air and makes everything smell fresh and wonderful.

Let me also say that although you may experience failures, it doesn't mean that you are a failure, any more than experiencing rain turns you into water.  Being a failure, or a success, is something that you experience; it's a part of the journey of life.

The five strategies of Part I are powerful; they can change your life.  Learn and follow them so you develop the right attitude about failures; so your eyes will be opened to see how the rain will bring spectacular success and abundance into your life.

# *Strategy 1.*

# *You are not a failure – but you must know how to recognize one.*

You will experience times of defeat, setbacks, problems, and adversity. You may have even been the cause of these things, but <u>you are never a failure</u>. Whenever you begin to feel discouraged by failure, remember that it is not you as a person that is the failure, it is always some <u>thing</u> which can be changed – such as a behavior, circumstance, or thought – that has produced disappointing results.

Each one of us is meant to succeed in life. It is our destiny. Henry David Thoreau said, "Men are born to succeed, not to fail." Success is your birthright. However, we must each choose that destiny. We will never be forced into having a happy and successful life. Even if others want it for us very badly, it is still a personal choice.

> *When you choose to be happy and successful, you will find happiness and success, but you needn't choose negativism and failure. It will find you on its own.*
>
> Napoleon Hill

You are never a failure, so long as you want to be a happy and successful person. Whether or not you experience success or failure is completely controlled by what you think and do. You are the only one who can choose the thoughts that will keep you from achieving the abundant life and joy that you are meant to have. No matter how difficult it may seem, say to yourself, "I choose to be a happy and successful person." That decision having been made, now read the rest of this strategy and learn how to recognize patterns of failure that can be changed by you as you learn how to manage your failures.

People often think that they are failures because they fall into a pattern of failing. They generally fall into three modes of failure. Sometimes they fail because they don't know what they desire in life and nothing that comes their way makes them happy. Others know what they want, but they don't know how to get what they want. And then there are those who know what they want and how to get it, but they don't know how to motivate themselves to do the things they know are necessary in order to be happy and successful.

I am going to explore each mode of failure so that you will be able to learn how to recognize all three of them when they occur in your life. Recognizing failure is like being able to determine your location, so you can plot a course to your ultimate destination. When I was learning how to navigate a ship, the instructors spent days, weeks, and even months showing us various ways to "fix" our position. I learned how to take bearings on lighthouses and other navigational aids and to use electronic navigational signals. I even was taught how to use a sextant on the sun and moon and various stars, so that I could determine a ship's exact location anywhere on earth.

Consider this to be a navigation lesson in which you learn how to "fix" where you are in life. By simply recognizing where you are in one of these three modes of failure, you will know where to start as you plan a course toward your success.

Failure Mode 1 – Not knowing what you desire in life.

*One of the most difficult things to do in life is think; that is why so few people engage in it.*
Henry Ford

Why do some people know what they want in life and others don't? I believe the difference is usually determined by whether people know their own mind. You were made in the image of God and the one and only thing that He gave you complete control over is your mind. If He gave you solitary control over your mind then we can be certain that He wants you to be in charge of your own mind. Thinking is work, so some people don't like to do it. But not all work has to be boring and unfulfilling.     The work of thinking can be fun and even adventurous.

For example, learning is thinking and learning can be a lot of fun. Unfortunately, many people have had the joy of learning drummed out of them at school. I know, because I was one of those persons. I finished school, not because I liked it, but because I wanted a good job. I didn't discover that learning was fun until later in life. If you are like me, let me tell you it is not too late. You do not need to be a college or even a high school graduate. All you have to do is find a subject or activity that you like and begin learning about it in a way that is fun. Here is how it happened to me.

I used to hate reading or even going into a library. Fortunately I was an engineer and engineers never had to use the library unless a research paper was assigned. I nearly flunked every course that involved reading or writing papers. Just after Cathy and I got married we moved to a small west coast town and I reported aboard my first ship. After we got there, Cathy said she wanted to visit the library to get a card. I thought she was crazy. We had just finished school. I asked her, "Why in the world would you want to go to the library? Do you want to do some research?" She said that the library had lots of fun books to read and she wanted to get some so when the ship was away she would have something to do in the evenings. I didn't offer to go with her.

Little by little my wife "tricked me" into reading. She knew I loved stories about Polynesia and the South Pacific. She borrowed a book written by James Michener called *Tales of the South Pacific*. When we went to bed she asked if she could read to me and of course I said yes. Just when we were getting to the good part she pretended that she was too tired to keep going, so I volunteered to continue. I was slow and I stumbled at first, but she encouraged me and corrected my awful pronunciation and helped me over words that I didn't know.

I eventually came to love books and reading, especially when Cathy escorted me to the library and showed me the do-it-yourself section. I thought I was in heaven. By learning to love books I could build or fix almost anything. No words can express my gratitude toward Cathy for doing that for me. Fortunately, you can benefit in the same way. Just go to the library or a large bookstore and start browsing some of your favorite topics. There are bound to be a couple of books that will captivate your interest.

When you become a learner, you can become a thinker. When you think, you take control of your mind and then you can dream. It has been medically proven that everyone has dreams when they sleep at night, whether they remember them or not. Everyone also has dreams when they are awake, but only about 1 out of every 3 people allow themselves to follow their dreams. It is difficult to say why. But one thing is for certain, if you do not let yourself dream of what you desire in life and give yourself permission to pursue those dreams, then you will not know true happiness.

Some people are afraid to dream because they feel limited by their past. Many of us think that the person we were yesterday has to be the same today. That just is not true. We have the capability to change with time. We are not tied to our past mistakes, habits, or limitations. Feeling that you cannot be SUCCESS BOUND today because you weren't yesterday is ridiculous and self-defeating. You can make an instant shift toward your success and abundant life by realizing that your life is lived moment by moment in a future direction, not controlled by the past.

> *For this is the journey that men make: to find themselves. If they fail in this, it doesn't matter much what else they find.*
>
> James Michener

Humans are the only created things that are allowed to change their habits; every other part of nature must continue with the same ones. Your habits are controlled by your mind, which we all know is changeable. If you take control of your mind, you can change your habits, then everything else in and around you is changeable. By changing your habits you can let go of the past. If you have been bound in mediocrity by looking at the past, then you can set yourself free by doing an "about face" and starting to live toward the future.  It will free you to pursue your dreams.

Sometimes people don't know what their own dreams are because they are too busy living other people's dreams.  There are times that you believe what others have told you, your spouse, parents, friends, business associates, and teachers; without really checking it out.  You may have factored these beliefs into major decisions in your life; such as your career, where you went to college, what jobs you took, or whom you married.  But people are all different, with differing dreams, hopes, desires, and goals.  If you want to find happiness and peace of mind, you need to follow your own dreams.

There is nothing wrong with listening to the advice of others, but you need to <u>know</u> what is best for you.  Don't be afraid to know your own mind, to know what you think.  When you know something, you feel it and it gives you a certainty about your beliefs.  There is wisdom within you; an intuition about what is best for you that you need to be aware of.  Try to spend some time each day in quiet thinking, even if it is for just a couple of minutes, so you can listen to your own inner self.  It is not selfish.  In fact, you will not be able to serve others in the way that you were meant to unless you do spend time getting to know your own mind.  It is said that when a man is introduced to himself, ties are broken and there are no longer any limitations on what he can achieve.  Not knowing yourself is a pattern of failure that can easily be broken.

There is a an old truism that goes like this; "You become what you think about most of the time."  If you think about success, you will form patterns of thought that will bring about opportunities and your abilities will be enhanced to be able to take on their challenges.  Conversely, if you think about failure and despair, you will not have the time or inclination to improve yourself.  Make a conscious decision now to think about what you desire in life.  Recognize negative thoughts and eliminate them by replacing them with their positive counterparts.

Failure Mode 2 – Not knowing how to get the success you desire.

> *People don't plan to fail, they fail to plan.*
> Old Adage

Why do some people get what they want and others fail? I believe that getting what you desire in life takes planning. It doesn't just happen by luck. It has been proven that successful people do things differently than unsuccessful people. Successful people recognize the patterns of success and follow them. One of those patterns of success is planning. Successful people plan what they think and do, which sets them apart. Therefore, you should learn how to plan for your success.

There have been reports of many people who have won the lottery jackpot, enjoyed luxuries for a short period of time, and then eventually gone back to their original level of poverty. Why? I believe it's because they didn't know how to plan for continued success. No one can predictably keep winning the lottery. Those who try and rely on luck for their success, lose it all and go back to where they started. Success does not like the gambler.

Successful people know exactly what they desire, have an intelligent plan for getting it, and then work their plan. They know what success will cost them in terms of time and energy and they devote the right resources toward making their plans happen. If you do not have a plan for how to succeed, then you have a plan for failing. A person whose life is out of control is someone without a definite plan. If that person is you then you can change that quickly by developing a plan for your life now.

Numerous books and audio tapes have been produced on how to develop personal plans. The one I recommend is Zig Ziglar's *Goals: Setting Them and Achieving Them On Schedule*. The five simplified steps that I follow are:

1) Decide on what you desire and write it down.
2) Determine the amount of time that you want to complete the goal.

3) Identify obstacles that must be overcome in order to achieve the goal.
4) Identify the resources (knowledge, skills, people, money, etc.) you have available already and those you must obtain.
5) Write out an action plan of the tasks to achieve the goal within the timeframe you allotted.

Another thing that successful people do differently from those who are tied to mediocrity is foster and maintain healthy relationships. Look around you and you will see that successful people express opinions to others after receiving all available information, which builds trust.   People who have failing relationships express opinions on subjects they know little about.  Successful people take a keen interest in others, especially those whom they have something in common with, and try to help others get what they want.  Losers try to get people to be their friend only when they want something from them.  Successful people have learned how to influence others through a cooperative attitude.  Unsuccessful people go out of their way to find fault and let others know about their critical attitude.  I could go on and on with examples.

> *I don't know the key to success, but the key to failure is trying to please everybody.*
> Bill Cosby

Several good books have been published on how to have and maintain good relationships.   One of the all-time best books on the subject is Dale Carnegie's *How To Win Friends & Influence People.* I highly recommend that it be on everyone's must-read list, even if you have read it before.  I have read it a number of times and I always pick up something new each time I read it.

Another book that I have found very valuable is *Boundaries*, by Drs. Henry Cloud and John Townsend.  They teach how to have a good understanding of psychological boundaries, because they define who a person is.  For example, you can immediately recognize someone who does not have healthy boundaries when they try to tell another person how to feel about something. People need to decide for themselves how they feel about something.

When you have healthy relationships you are able to enlist the help of others. None of us can be successful on our own. We all need the help of others. Therefore, successful people learn how to earn the trust and respect of others. If you have a difficult time with relationships, resolve now to learn how to change so that people will be drawn to you and want to cooperate with you. Strategy 2 covers some of the things that you can do in order to improve your character traits so that people will find you more attractive.

### Failure Mode 3 – Not knowing how to motivate yourself to obtain the success you desire.

Why do some people always seem to be upbeat and positive about the future and in control of their lives, while others see only doom and gloom ahead? I believe that having a passion for living comes from learning how to appropriate passion and positive emotions in your life. People are not just born happy. It is a learned response. I'm sure a lot of it has to do with early childhood development, but it has been proven that it is not a permanent condition. People can learn how to be happy. As Americans, we believe that the 'pursuit of happiness' is an *inalienable right* of each person. But how do you pursue happiness? Let's look at just some of the ways that people obtain the passion in life that motivates them to be successful.

> *Whatsoever thy hand findeth to do, do it with all thy might.*
> Ecclesiastes

I heard a statement once that I agree with; "Happiness is loving what you do and getting paid for it." Several other authors have confirmed this saying. One of the most popular is Marsha Sinetar, who wrote *Do What You Love, the Money Will Follow*. Accomplishing your major purpose in life brings a sense of fulfillment and when you are passionate for what you do, success will follow. Work becomes its own reward.

A few years ago I was working in the Coast Guard, but it lacked personal congruence; which is mind, body, and spirit enthusiastically moving toward abundant life. Working hard showed no inward reward. I borrowed Marsha's book from the library. The beginning was lukewarm, but I soon realized some hot, freeing insights. I wasn't being rewarded inwardly because I was working hard in the wrong livelihood; not using my innate talents to their fullest. It set me on a quest. It is a mission that I highly recommend to you. Find what you like to do and what you are good at; they usually are the same, given the right level of attention. Doing what you love gets you working eagerly and joyfully. It takes courage, but it is worth it. When people see me now in my proper career they usually comment on my high energy level. I'm complimented for "working hard," but it's more like I'm having a ball.

Permanent happiness and financial freedom can be yours, but only if you are satisfied with the important aspects of your life, particularly your work, since that is where so much of your time is spent. You can achieve satisfaction by learning how to take charge of your own destiny and developing a positive faith in yourself and your abilities. The key to doing what you love and loving what you do is in becoming a positive, focused, self-confident and goal-oriented person. It can make the difference between dreaming about life and living your dream.

Even if you can't do what you love right now, learn how to reward yourself more often with what you love. Figure out how to make it the reward that you give yourself for doing the things you have to do for now. Don't keep pushing your personal happiness off into the nebulous future. It will suck the passion out of your life and leave you feeling empty.

The vast majority of people's emotions are based on the type of thinking they do. When it comes to the factors that determine whether or not they have happiness and abundant life, I believe that there are two basic modes of thinking: <u>reactive</u> and <u>proactive</u>.

The reactive thinkers often make quick and poorly thought-out decisions; therefore, they feel the pressure of stress and lose perspective.  They take things personally and get annoyed with themselves, bothered by others, and frustrated when things don't go well.  Being reactive produces a downward spiral that brings out the worst in them.  Other people begin to be annoyed with their overly critical and negative attitudes.  They are rigid and inflexible.  They never have time to take advantage of opportunities when they knock because they are so wrapped up with their problems.

However, when you take on a proactive frame of mind you see things differently.  When you are a proactive thinker, you are more relaxed because you are looking ahead to the future and making decisions that meet most, if not all, of your objectives in life.  You are in control and have your bearings.  You take things less personally because you see the big picture and understand how everything interacts.  You are flexible and calm, take full responsibility for the results of your actions, and then make adjustments quickly so the next time you will be more successful.  You look for ways to bring out the best in others and enjoy their full cooperation when needed.  Your eyes are open to opportunities and your mind is tuned in, ready to take on the challenge.

> *The thing always happens that you really believe in; and the belief in a thing makes it happen.*
> Frank Lloyd Wright

The results of these two different ways of thinking are predictable and often drastic.  Begin to notice which frame of mind you are in, and then you will be able to stop yourself from drifting into the irrational reactive mode that produces failures.  You will be able to wisely choose the more beneficial proactive state of mind.

Proactive thinking is a combination of positive thinking, systematic thinking, futuristic thinking, and intelligent thinking.  Simply becoming aware of how to think more proactively will open up your life to beneficial changes.  You will begin to feel more in control of your mind and therefore your entire life.  You will become impatient with yourself when you fall into the reactive frame of mind, which will trigger a shift back to being more proactive.

Stephen Covey, one of my favorite authors, has become known as a modern day Socrates. In his book, *The 7 Habits of Highly Effective People,* he describes "being proactive" as the first habit toward being effective. In actuality, it is the foundational principle of effectiveness, because it gives substance to all of the other habits. Covey's keen insight into linking personal responsibility with the proactive approach opened up a whole new world to me. I gained a higher level of understanding that has changed my life. I believe that I am a walking testimony of the goodness of his philosophies. You will experience far greater rewards when you choose the proactive approach. This type of reward will help you to change from reactive to proactive thinking. A proactive state of mind is more conducive to happiness and abundance – the true riches of life. An added bonus is that others will truly enjoy being around you.

> *Look at the word responsibility – 'response-ability' – the ability to choose your response. Highly proactive people recognize that responsibility. They do not blame circumstances, conditions, or conditioning for their behavior. Their behavior is a product of their own conscious choice ...*
> Stephen Covey

When your mind is relaxed and free from worries of failure, you turn on passion and create a burning desire to accomplish your major purpose in life. When you have a deep-rooted passion, you will have a sincerity that will make you unstoppable. When you are unstoppable, you will achieve your goals and eventually realize what you desire and deserve. Start right now by deciding to become a proactive thinker and then use the power of proactive thinking to create your own success. You are responsible.

You are not a failure, but now you know how to <u>recognize patterns of failures</u> in your life. You must be successful at knowing what you want, knowing how to get it, and motivating yourself to make it happen. If you only have two out of these three, your life will be out of balance; you will most likely remain bound to mediocrity. Be truthful with yourself and admit where you might be coming up short. It will trigger a winning attitude that will start you racing toward a life that has rainbows after the rain.

✓ *Know what you desire in life. Know your dreams, ambitions, talents, and gifts. Don't be afraid to know your own mind and to enjoy learning.*

✓ *Know how to get what you desire in life. Successful people have certain key life skills; planning is one that you should acquire as soon as possible. Additionally, learn how to have good relationships because we all need the help of others.*

✓ *Know how to motivate yourself to obtain the success you desire. Build passion by doing what you love to do. Become a proactive thinker – rewards will follow.*

# Strategy 2.

## Always fail forward toward your goals.

It has been said that, "the only true failure in life is the person who doesn't know what he or she wants, because no path will bring true happiness." It is a travesty to me to see the great numbers of people who live their lives without any sense of purpose. They seem to work at jobs as if bound by the chains of mediocrity, and think that God has unjustly withheld His blessing from them, or, that any one else who has achieved more success than them has just been lucky.

Mediocrity doesn't just affect the poor. I have observed that lack of purpose affects people with a wide range of income levels. In fact, those who earn a larger paycheck because they are better educated can afford to buy lots of things, but often don't have the things that money can't buy, like happiness, good relationships, and peace of mind. They have become failures at living, not because they fail, but because they don't fail toward their purpose in life and thereby learn to be successful in all areas.

> *When life gives you lemons, make lemonade and then sell it to all of those who get thirsty from complaining.*
> Napoleon Hill

The importance of having a purpose in life cannot be over-emphasized. Having a definite purpose simplifies the process of planning and makes the hundreds of decisions that need to be made far easier. A definite purpose gives you the reason to keep going when the going gets difficult. It gives you courage to try new things out and to stretch your comfort zone until it surrounds all of the things that are important to you.

I recall one event that happened to our family that demonstrates the importance of purpose. Our experience was similar to another family's, yet the outcome for each family was exactly the opposite – a full 180 degrees out.

In 1991 I was fortunate enough to get assigned to the Coast Guard Marine Safety Office on the Island of Oahu, in Hawaii. Our assigned house was not ready so the government put us up temporarily at a hotel on Waikiki for six weeks, room and meals paid for. WOW, who could ask for more? We could pretend to be rich tourists and not have to pay extra to be there.

Since we were home-schooling our children, school was always in session, so my wife found out about everything that was going on in Waikiki and made the most of it. For six weeks, my children took free hula and ukulele (a small guitar-like instrument) lessons. They visited dozens of beach sites and learned all about the tropical sea life. They found discounted merchandise and got a head start on all of our extended family Christmas gifts. My wife and I were able to enjoy many of the restaurants and some of the nightlife. To us it was like heaven on earth, or at least an extended honeymoon.

The other family had almost the identical setting but at a slightly different time. When we met them later at a social event, we could not believe our ears. They had nothing good to say about their Waikiki experience – it was all complaint.

They had three children just like us but did not have plans to educate them or help them enjoy Hawaii. They didn't get out and see anything in particular and when they did venture out a little, it was disappointing because they didn't make the effort to see what was available. They got sick of staying in a hotel and eating the same food, even complaining about being served coffee, tea, and pastries every morning. It was as if they were forced to endure a Siberian prison rather than a hotel with tourists who were paying a lot of their own hard-earned money so they could enjoy a tropical paradise for a few days. They said they were afraid to venture too far because they were afraid of getting lost. The fear of failure can hold people back from enjoying life, even in paradise.

It was ironic that they thought we just had a lucky experience. But it wasn't luck! We had a definite purpose of teaching our children from every experience and we made plans to take advantage of our situation. We were not afraid to get out and find out what we liked and didn't like. We planned to have a good time and WE DID!

My advice to you is to work very hard at knowing what you "want." For knowing what you want is at least half of the effort required to achieving what you want. When you know what you want, even when you fail, you can at least fail in the right direction. You will have a learning experience that teaches you more of what you need to know to be successful. So after a knockdown, you can get right back up and take the next step or two toward your goal. Almost all of life is two steps forward and one step back. However, if you make sure that the two steps forward are in the direction that you want to go, you just might find that even when you slip up, you will be failing in the right direction.

**Discover your major purpose in life.**

> *There is no greater force on this earth than a man with a purpose.*
> Anonymous

How do you discover what you desire in life; what really brings you abundant life and joy? I believe that you should break it down into three elements: DO, BE, and HAVE, in that order.

**What is it that you were meant to DO?** Everyone has been created for a purpose; what is yours? Some refer to it as a "calling." In fact the Bible says, "many are called but few are chosen." I believe that this means everyone is called, but only a few choose to heed the calling. Since they are the ones willing, they are the ones chosen. Some people find this to be a very difficult struggle. One of the best books that I have ever read on the subject is by Laurie Beth Jones. In her book, *The Path – Creating your Mission Statement for Work and for Life,* Laurie Beth helps people discover their "mission in life." She then provides guidance in how to express it, mainly by writing it out, so that it can be used as a tool to focus your thoughts and activities to achieve success.

I sometimes tell people that discovering their major purpose is like finding the perfect marriage partner. You engage in similar thoughts and action as when you fall in love with the one who was "meant to be." We don't normally expect someone to pick our partner for us, or wait until God supernaturally points the person out. Even Joseph of Nazareth fell in love with Mary and got engaged, and then he was chosen to be the earthly "Father of Jesus."

I believe that most people know what they are "meant to do," even if it is just an inkling. For some reason, I was afraid to act upon my definite major purpose for quite a long time. I was afraid that I would fail at it. If you have a fear of acting upon your major purpose in life, please carefully read Strategy 12 on how to rid yourself of the fear of failure.

There is a question that is commonly asked, in almost a joking manner, of career military people, "What are you going to do when you grow up?" I struggled with this for quite awhile. I joined the Coast Guard at the age of 17, not knowing what I was meant to do. I was educated very well as a shipboard engineer and a naval architect. However, as I began learning the science of personal achievement, I discovered my true major purpose was far more than ship design and operation.

I learned that I was meant to fully understand the principles of being proactive, so that I could help businesses and individuals perform at their optimum levels of achievement in service quality and safety. After reading *The Path*, I was able to write my mission statement in this way, "I learn, live and teach the principles of proactive thinking in order to help bring abundant life to all."

After a lot of thought and contemplation, I realized that the kind of improvements that I was compelled to recommend to the marine industry were not the kind that could be brought about by regulations. My "calling" has led me to retire from the Coast Guard. I describe it as getting on the other end of the rope so I could start pulling with the industry, instead of pushing it around.

> Drifting, without aim or purpose, is the first cause of failure.
> Napoleon Hill

Of course not everyone is meant to leave the Coast Guard. At my retirement ceremony I remarked that I had joined the Coast Guard to get a good education and after 22 years I felt like I was finally graduating. It wasn't that I was a slower learner, but rather that I had different, more challenging, lessons to learn. If you do not know your definite major purpose in life, then make it your goal to find out what it is so that you can fail forward. I promise you that you will never regret it.

**What is it that you were meant to BE?** The answer to this question largely depends on what you are meant to do. For, in order to be very good at what you do, you must have certain essential knowledge, skills, character traits and values. If you are meant to be the best golfer in the world, then you are going to have to BE – a golfer.

When I was working for the Coast Guard as a naval architect, I was able to be a very good one by being a typical engineer kind of person. I was very much like Scott Adams' *Dilbert*, who is one of my favorite cartoon characters. I did not have to be an outgoing salesman or business manager. I had to BE an engineer to be successful.

Identifying myself as a Christian, I have always had a strong set of values and virtues, which helped bolster my Coast Guard career as an officer and leader. However, since discovering my major purpose, I found that I could no longer just be an engineer. I needed to improve almost every other success factor so that I could BE a writer, speaker, business consultant, and trainer. I went to work building myself up by reading dozens of books, attending seminars, listening to tapes, watching videos, and of course practicing, practicing, practicing. I found tapes from Nightingale-Conant Corporation to be invaluable in that regard, allowing my car to become a "Success University."

> *A winner is someone who recognizes his God-given talents, works his tail off to develop them into skills, and uses these skills to accomplish his goals.*
>
> Larry Bird

If you know what it is that you were meant to do, make a list of the things that you now need to BE, so you can get good at what you do. Look for the key success factors or the core competencies that you must have incorporated into your life in order to get good at what you have to BE. What knowledge and level of skill must you have? Where are you going to get your education and the experience you will need? What are the virtues, values, and character traits that you should have?

In his research, Napoleon Hill discovered that there are 25 common character traits that all successful people exhibit. They are listed in *Napoleon Hill's Keys to Success – The 17 Principles of Personal Achievement.* Similarly, Ben Franklin, an ordinary printer, became a founding father of our country and one of the most influential statesmen to ever have lived. He had 13 virtues that he felt would be most helpful to him. The following are values, character traits and virtues I feel are most important for myself. However, it would be worth your effort to write out your own list based on the type of person you want to become.

1. *Love and serve others by living my mission.*
2. *Be a proactive decision maker.*
3. *Develop a positive mental attitude based on faith and hope.*
4. *Have a pleasant tone of voice and speak frankly.*
5. *Make a habit of smiling and using friendly facial expressions.*
6. *Be tolerant and understanding of others' points of view.*
7. *Be goal and future oriented.*
8. *Always use appropriate words and effective speech.*
9. *Use courtesy and tact in all business situations.*

10.  *Show fondness for people and use a good handshake upon greeting.*

11.  *Develop traits of sportsmanship, showmanship, and personal magnetism.*

12.  *Maintain a high sense of integrity and Biblical morals.*

13.  *Be frugal toward self and generous toward others.*

If your values or character traits are out of balance from what they should be, then you have a gap in part of your life that needs to be closed.  If you feel that your life has never been in balance, don't panic, most of us feel that way.  The steps to follow are not that difficult.  I use a modified version of Ben Franklin's approach.  I believe it is simple, yet very powerful.  Here it is written out as I understand and use it.

> *A good character is, in all cases, the fruit of personal exertion.  It is not inherited from parents; it is not created by external advantages; it is no necessary appendage of birth, wealth, talents, or station; but it is the result of one's own endeavors – the fruit and reward of good principles manifested in a course of virtuous and honorable action.*
> J. Hawes

Enumerate the names of the values, virtues, and character traits that are necessary or desirable.  Write them with a short precept to fully express their meaning.  Organize them in such a way that acquiring a first might facilitate acquiring the second and the subsequent.  Acquire the habit of these virtues by fixing your attention on each one for a period of time in turn.  Perhaps try only a week at a time until you have gone through them at least once.  For best affect, when you have rotated through them, return to the beginning.

Ben Franklin wrote in his autobiography, "I entered upon the execution of this plan for self-examination, and was surprised to find myself so much fuller of faults than I had imagined, but I had the satisfaction of seeing them diminish."  It worked for Ben and it can work for you.

Frank Bettger, a very successful insurance salesman in the early half of the last century, wrote in his book, *How I Raised Myself From Failure To Success In Selling,* that he used the same approach with great results. Bettger of course customized the virtues to fit what he needed to excel at in order to be a top-notch salesman. You must do the same with your list of values, virtues, and character traits. This method can help you improve in just about any area of your life, including skills that you believe are needed in order to be successful at your major purpose in life.

There is one character trait that will automatically be increased just by acting upon your major purpose in life – that is sincerity. When you set goals toward becoming very good at your major purpose you will have a higher level of sincerity. You will BE sincere because you will have a sincere desire to serve others by doing what you are passionate about. Napoleon Hill said, "Sincerity is a trait that pays off in self-satisfaction, self-respect and the spiritual ability to live with ourselves twenty-four hours a day."

Another significant advantage of having sincerity that I have discovered is that it becomes a shield against adversity. "When the going gets tough, the tough get going" is a phrase that describes Coast Guard search and rescue units. It seems they are always heading out to sea when everyone else is coming in. They have a definite purpose – a mission. The sincerity with which those brave men and women perform their job is their shield against the most adverse conditions – it can be yours too. You can achieve whatever goal you set so long as you have a sincere desire to accomplish your major purpose and serve others. When you are sincere you will BE courageous.

**What is it that you are meant to HAVE?** Similar to the section above, the answer to this question largely depends on what you were meant to do and be. If you are a real estate agent, then you will want to HAVE – a nice car. You will be a much better agent if you can drive prospective buyers around in a nice car that is comfortable, shows that you have good taste, and indicates that you care about them as clients.

> *If you have a definite purpose in life, the word impossible can be struck from your vocabulary – for it has become a word without a meaning.*
>
> Anonymous

Zig Ziglar, America's number one motivational speaker, gives one of my favorite quotes, "Strive to get all of the things money can't buy and just some of the things money can buy." This has been a guiding principle in my life since I've heard it. I recommend you make it yours too. I believe Zig's saying is based on the words of Jesus; "Worry not about what you should eat or drink or what you should wear, for your Heavenly Father knows you need all of these things, but seek first the kingdom of God and all of these things will be given to you."

Do not seek to become rich in money only, but to be rich in the greatest riches of life, the riches that come from what money cannot buy. If you expect the riches of money alone to bring you happiness, you will be sorely disappointed. You will only acquire anxiety, misery, and fear. Money can be a great blessing if you work to acquire it by serving others. I believe that work is not only essential for happiness and true prosperity, but it is a form of worship, because it is expressing your gifts and talents in such a way that makes your "Heavenly Father" very happy.

By the *Law of Abundance*, you will have your fill, to the point of satisfaction, of whatever your needs might be. While wandering in the desert, the Bible says the Israelites received manna in "unlimited" amounts every day, except for the Sabbath. They were told to gather as much as they needed for each person to have his fill, but no more, otherwise it would spoil. Those who didn't trust the *Law of Abundance*, and took a little extra, wound up with a tent full of worms the next morning – YUCK! The Israelites learned to take only as much as was enough to satisfy the appetite of each person.

Everyone has a different appetite, both for type and amount of food; the key is to learn how to recognize when you HAVE "enough." My son's favorite type of restaurant is any restaurant that has "All You Can Eat" on the menu. He has a significant appetite to match his high metabolism and he likes to be able to eat his fill. There have been times when he was younger that we had to caution him to remember his limit, but it always amazed us how much it was.

I believe that the same is true for your appetite for money and other wealth. Everyone has a certain appetite for it based on the kind of person that they are meant to be. In order to enjoy happiness and peace of mind you need to learn to acquire just enough. Take a proactive approach toward discovering your appetite. Optimize your wealth based on what your major purpose is and the person you are meant to be. Mother Teresa would not be happy driving a Cadillac Seville. That is not what she would want to HAVE. If you were meant to be a great real estate agent you would not be happy to HAVE an ox-drawn cart.

| |
|---|
| *Waste not –* |
| *Want not.* |
| Ben Franklin |

I am convinced that there will never be an end to our resources so long as we manage them and recognize our appetites. Your appetite for wealth might be large, for others it might be small. What is important to note is that God knows your needs and has made provision for you to have your fill.

Napoleon Hill, author of the hugely successful book *Think and Grow Rich*, which was based on a lifetime of research into the science of personal achievement said, "A failure has no definite purpose in life and believes that all success is the result of luck. The successful people know precisely what they desire, have a plan for getting it, believe in their abilities to get it, and devote major portions of their time acquiring it."

Follow your passion and major purpose. If you do not have a major purpose in life, then you will be either tied to mediocrity or drifting about aimlessly in a sea of confusion. Even if you motor about, steering from one part of the sea to another, you are in danger. Without a chart and compass to guide you, you are in grave danger of being cast upon a reef somewhere and losing everything.

You must know and follow the *Law of Purpose* – which simply says that every created thing has a purpose. You will become a much happier and more prosperous person if you discover your major purpose and then begin learning how to get really good at it. We are all created beings, sharing the universal purpose of having a relationship with God and living harmoniously with the rest of creation. We must each get to know Him, and then follow His special purpose for us.

> *I know that there is nothing better for man than to rejoice and to do good in one's lifetime, moreover, that every man who eats and drinks sees good in all his labor – it is the gift of God.*
>
> King Solomon

Everyone has his or her own major purpose in life. In the Book of Psalms it says, "God gives us the desires of our heart." I believe that means He both puts the desires within your heart and then works everything for your good so that your desires can be fulfilled. Everyone has a calling, but not everyone chooses to listen to that calling.

I've run into many people who are afraid to believe they are called because they think that God's only desire for them would be for them to become missionaries. I smile and tell them that that is not the case and if more people would believe, then the need for missionaries would be a whole lot less.

Know your mind; let your inner wisdom speak to you. You will discover how to ensure your skies are filled with spectacular rainbows, and how to have the abundant life and joy that really makes you feel like a success, by discovering what it is that you are meant to DO, BE, and HAVE. Give yourself permission to make mistakes, to let yourself fail at first, while you are pursuing that major purpose in life, which gives you passion. You only have one life, make it a good one.

✓ *Discover your passion – what you are meant to DO. It can bring you <u>all</u> of the things money can't buy; peace of mind, happiness, loving relationships, etc. Living your passion will make life more enjoyable for you and your family.*

✓ *Look within yourself and see what kind of person you need to BE in order to fulfill your life purpose, then make a plan to become that person.*

✓ *Be practical and choose what things you would like to HAVE that will support you and increase your passion for fulfilling your definite major purpose in life.*

# Strategy 3.

## Be Prepared for the Worst Failure

On her maiden voyage, the passenger liner TITANIC was not prepared for the worst failure. The owners thought it to be unsinkable, but it only had enough lifeboats for less than half the persons on board. The naval architect had done his engineering homework and had the collision been an ordinary one with another ship, the TITANIC would in all probability have survived. The designer planned out as best he could a ship that wouldn't sink <u>and</u> he planned the upper deck to be large enough for sufficient lifeboats to carry 100% of the people on board.

The owner however, did not follow through and prepare for the worst failure, purportedly because too much of the upper deck would have been taken up with another row of lifeboats on either side of the ship. The lessons in marine safety that the world learned from the TITANIC were enormous. In fact, the Court of Inquiry set the stage for the first International Convention for the Safety of Life at Sea (SOLAS). That Convention was the beginning of the shipping rules we depend on today to have clean oceans and safe and enjoyable vacations on large passenger cruise ships.

> *The best preparation for the future is the present well seen to, and the last duty done.*
> G. MacDonald

There is a lesson for you to learn from the TITANIC disaster too. Here is the key to managing your failures: "If you are prepared for the worst possible event, it usually won't happen, and even if it does happen, you can confidently know that all will not be lost." You can know that even if the dreaded failure occurs and your ship is about to sink, you can simply put on your lifejacket and climb safely aboard your lifeboat.

When George W. Bush's father, the first President Bush, jumped from his burning plane in 1944, it was not without a parachute. Engineers have learned the valuable lesson of making provisions for the worst failure, thus giving the pilot a fighting chance of survival. If they didn't do that, our pilots would always be holding back and not fully engaging the enemy. You must do the same for yourself if you are to fully be engaged in the pursuit of success. Allow – and even plan for – the time when you will need a parachute or a lifejacket. You need to think ahead and prepare for the worst possible failure.

I am a naval architect and I have a lot of experience in the U.S. Coast Guard writing safety regulations for ships. The primary focus of the regulations is on preventing accidents. However, many of the safety regulations force the marine industry to plan for the eventuality of a failure. It ensures that any potential harm emanating from a failure will be contained. It is commonly known that no matter how safe the ship is designed to be, there is always the chance that an accident could occur that was bigger than anticipated. Therefore, the Coast Guard requires the industry to plan for the worst failure when designing a boat or ship.

The following is a 3-tiered planning process that is used for writing safety regulations. These steps are also appropriate for designing your life's pursuits and planning your goals so you can "safely" achieve success.

> *You must plan - but you must not follow your first plan; for no plan was ever perfect when first conceived, and so if it were followed without improvement, it would guarantee a less than perfect result.*
>
> Randy Gilbert

**Plan A** is develop the normal plans for your life that will lead to "successful" conditions using the resources that are available. You should clarify your objectives, analyze the resources available, and take steps to accomplish the goals that will meet your objectives. It is not always simple. A ship designer has hundreds of variables to consider that ensure a ship can be operated profitably and safely. Don't be discouraged if life seems complicated to you, just keep on working on a plan that will ultimately bring about success.

**Plan B** is set up a containment plan should something go awry. Containing the harmful situation so that it can go no further is sometimes called "hedging." It is like setting up protective boundaries that help to contain and protect your resources should Plan A fail. For instance, no one plans for shipboard fires, but they happen. An unadvertised fact is that unwanted fires occur on large passenger cruise ships almost every day. Therefore, a modern cruise ship is built so that a fire can be contained to a small area until it is extinguished – which is almost always the case.

**Plan C** is your emergency escape plan. If Plan B fails and the hazard cannot be contained, there must be a way to preserve the critical resources of your life. On a cruise ship there are many fireproof bulkheads to contain a fire if it starts. But, if the fire were to burn hot and out of control and spread to more areas of the ship, the passengers might need to be evacuated. Therefore, all cruise ships sailing now must have an "abandon ship" plan and enough lifeboats or rafts to save all of the lives of the people on board if the ship is no longer a safe place to remain.

It would be very uncomfortable and restrictive to have to wear a lifejacket for the whole time you were on a cruise ship – it is meant to be worn only during emergencies. So when must you put on your lifejacket? Once you realize that you have come to the point when it seems as if all will be lost, you need to put your lifejacket on securely and get into the lifeboat.

I have not gone through a complete financial disaster yet, but I have read of those who have. Some people are crushed by it. Their lives seem to be ruined. They hid from what they saw coming, lied to others and to themselves about it, and refused to take responsibility for their actions. Who would help them or even talk to them now? Because they neglected saving their integrity, they lost their own trustworthiness and remain unable to recover.

> *Happy are those who knowing they are subject to uncertain changes, are prepared and armed for either fortune; a rare principle, and with much labor learned in wisdom's school.*
>                                    Massinger

On the other hand, some people rebound after financial disaster even higher than before. It seems they are able to cling to their self-respect, hope and personal integrity. Thus they keep safe from complete failure. They gather up what is left of their lives, and then use the new understanding they received from the disaster to make positive plans for beginning anew. Your lifejacket is made of two essential things that will buoy you when all else is lost: 1) the power of your mind to know what's right, and 2) the freedom to choose it.

By remembering to cling to self-respect, hope and personal integrity you will always be able to start again. You may not have the money or the friends you once had. But if you know what your purpose in life is and you have a burning desire to serve others by it, then you cannot be stopped. You can be confident that, by the *Law of Compensation*, the Creator of the universe will reward you for your honest efforts of service. When you gain a greater understanding of how to avoid making the same mistakes, your chances of succeeding are much higher than someone else who has not had the same experience. Remember to prepare Plans A, B, and C and you will be ready to boldly give it all you've got – your success will be guaranteed – rainbows will come out after the rain.

✓ *Proactively plan your responses before you are tested by a failure. Develop Plan A so your normal operating condition is optimum success.*

✓ *Develop Plan B so you can limit failures to one area of your life and prevent the out-of-control situation from happening.*

✓ *Develop Plan C as your 'abandon ship' response. Maintain a high level of integrity so your powerful mind will always be available to buoy you up and point to success, no matter what happens.*

# Strategy 4.

# Find the root cause of persistent failures.

Despite your best efforts, there will be times of defeat, setbacks, problems, and adversity. Sometimes problems will persist. Do not be discouraged by failures that don't seem to go away at first. As I said in the beginning, it is not you as a person who is a failure; it is always some <u>thing</u> that can be changed. It may be that you have been dealing with a symptom of the problem and not the root cause of the problem itself.

A number of years ago I was mowing our lawn on a hot summer day and I was wearing shorts. I did not know it at the time but some poison ivy had taken root in our yard next to the fence line. During a break I remember scratching the back of my right leg with the toe of my left shoe. What followed shortly thereafter was an awful case of a poison ivy rash. I tried to get rid of the problem rash by using benadryl cream on my skin and by taking benadryl tablets. The rash persisted and seemed to get worse. I was miserable. I went to the doctor. He said that because of my scratching with the shoe, I had a case of poison ivy that was systemic. He prescribed some mild steroids and additional creams. It began to work and within a week I was back to normal.

> *It is impossible to solve significant problems using the same knowledge that created them.*
> Albert Einstein

So, did the problem rash stay gone? No, of course not; the next time I mowed the lawn it was back! I had dealt with the poison ivy rash for good, I thought, but it was a symptom. The root cause of the problem – the real problem – was nasty poison ivy plants that quickly grew new leaves.

I had to educate myself as to what they looked like, where they were, and then, how to get rid of them. With the proper weed killer and medicine the whole problem went away. I also volunteered to solve the problem over in my neighbor's lawn so the poison ivy would stay away.

Failures give us the opportunity to learn from unexpected results. When the result is not the one you intended, then you can make adjustments until you do achieve the desired results. When you experience persistent failures it is usually because there is a deep-rooted cause that has not been fully dealt with. You need to learn what that root cause is so you can then learn how to remove it.

## The Right Tools

My father taught me that I should always choose the right tool for the job. Whether I am fixing my old truck or solving a business problem, that rule has been very helpful to me. It is important to have a good set of tools so that you will be able to choose the right one when the time comes.

I will identify some tools that will help to detect the root causes to various types of problems, so you can acquire the tools and add them to your own toolbox. I recommend that you continue to collect tools that will be helpful to you and will be available when the need arises.

There are two basic categories of detection tools: *reactive* and *proactive*. The reactive tools are those that usually come at the end of an event or process. They leave little time, if any, to make adjustments before the process is complete. Therefore, resources such as energy, time, and money are wasted when a problem occurs.

Reactive tools come after the value added activity. They are usually inspection oriented and are implemented with minimum thought or effort. That is why they tend to be more widely used.

To illustrate an example, picture in your mind a print shop where business cards are made. There are several distinct processes:

order taking, billing, typesetting & layout, plate making, printing, and finally slitting and boxing. Each process must be working properly in order for the cards to turn out to meet the customer's expectations. .

If the shop owner only implements a reactive detection method of inspection, which is usually the customer checking the cards as he pays for them, we can all guess that this print shop will be fraught with problems and complaints. Failures will mean dissatisfied customers, not just incorrect business cards. Since reprints will eat up most of the profit, it probably won't be in business long.

> *Your failure may prove to be an asset, provided you know why you failed.*
> Napoleon Hill

Proactive detection tools, on the other hand, can be used as a part of the event or process. They are often interconnected with the processes so they can be used to make timely adjustments in order to conserve resources. They are usually self-assessment and audit oriented, which require a clear set of objectives. Proactive detection tools generally require more effort to implement, but they can save time and money if used properly.

Let's continue the above print shop example and see how proactive detection methods could be put in place to ensure customer satisfaction. Start by having the person who is taking the order double check all of the details on the order form with the customer, including billing, to make sure it is fully understood and legible. From my personal experience, this one proactive step would eliminate about 50% of the potential customer dissatisfaction problems. The person doing the typesetting and layout process should also be required to reread his work. Both of these steps are inexpensive and very effective.

When the typesetter is done he passes the layout with the order form to the plate maker, so she can also double-check the typesetter's work before making the plate. Similarly, the plate maker passes the order form with the plates to the pressman so he can double-check the set-up work and choose the right paper and ink colors. The slitter gets the order form so she can double-check the alignment and quantity before the cards are slit and boxed.

> *Difficulty is the soil in which all manly and womanly qualities best flourish; and the true worker, in any sphere, is continually coping with difficulties. His very failures, throwing him upon his own resources, cultivate energy and resolution; his hardships teach him fortitude; his successes inspire self-reliance. It cannot be too often repeated that it is not helps, but obstacles; not facilities, but difficulties that make men.*
>
> W. Mathews

This type of proactive detection is set up as teamwork and is focused on fixing the problems – not the blame. Everyone realizes how their job impacts the other people down the line and more importantly, how what they do is linked with satisfying the customer. It also makes it very easy to find and correct mistakes in a cost-effective manner.

Although this illustration is a type of manufacturing process, the concepts can be applied to just about any situation. I've been working on improving my public speaking abilities. I have learned that everything about speaking counts, no matter how small the detail – it either helps or hurts.

In his book, *The Quick & Easy Way to Effective Speaking,* Dale Carnegie tells of assisting two brothers many years ago who gained notoriety by flying from London to Australia. He helped them prepare an illustrated travel talk of the flight. Although he trained them both in its delivery, one was far more successful than the other at public speaking.

Here is what Dale Carnegie wrote as a part of his explanation of how the little things make the difference. "They had had identically the same experience, they had sat side by side as they flew halfway around the world, and they delivered the same talk, almost word for word. Yet, somehow it didn't sound like the same talk at all."

Napoleon Hill had the following saying, "Don't overlook small details. Remember that the universe and all that is in it are made from tiny atoms." He taught that every job is made up of smaller ones, which if ignored, can create problems.

Another truism is, "When you take care of the little things, the big things will take care of themselves." Dale Carnegie outlines in his books all of the things that are important to public speaking. I can see how I need to pay attention to all of them. I am setting up a proactive way of ensuring the details are remembered so I can make improvements to my speeches. If I were to rely on my audience to be the only problem detector, then I would be in the reactive mode. I would be certain to make mistakes that the audience would notice. Then I would have the double misfortune of not satisfying my audience and I would not be able to find the true cause of their dissatisfaction.

> *You can take the advice of one of the greatest minds this continent has ever produced, Benjamin Franklin. I know exactly what he would say if it were possible for you to sit down alongside of him today and ask his advice. He would tell you to take one thing at a time, and give a week's strict attention to that one thing; leaving all the others to their ordinary chance.*
> Frank Bettger

If you are a salesman, you might consider all of the various small tasks that need to be done associated with prospecting, presenting, closing, and following-up. A less experienced salesman might dismiss some tasks as unimportant details, but we know that true success will elude him.

In his book, *How I Raised Myself From Failure to Success In Selling*, Frank Bettger outlines many details, all of which when taken together made him very successful. I believe you can have the same type of success if you follow through with learning all of the important details of your business, and then setting up a proactive way of ensuring they are implemented as a part of your daily routine.

When I have a problem with a process, I divide the process into four categories in order to more easily find the root cause of the problem. The categories are commonly referred to as the four M's: *Man, Method, Machine,* and *Materials*.

The first two – Man and Method – are "software" related. *Man* covers all of the aspects of people such as education, training, skill level, and experience. *Method* covers how the process is planned out and implemented. It includes such things as the order of events, controls, and layout of the workspace.

The second two – Machine and Materials – are "hardware" related. *Machine* covers all of the equipment that is involved and includes checking for appropriateness, maintenance, and reliability. *Materials* include all of the non-people resources that are needed in the process. For example, if the process is making a shirt, it is important to select the right kind of fabric for the type of shirt being made.

I also find it helpful to consider the correlation between *Man* and *Machine,* which includes ergonomics, human factors, and fit. For instance, does a worker constantly have to reach or bend over to use the machine properly? Additionally, I review the correlation between *Man* and *Method*, which covers appropriate competence level and behavioral styles of the people involved. A ship designer needs to consider the appropriate competence level for each position on the ship during its operation.

When setting up a new process, the best thing to do is establish some manner of a proactive detection method. You should have some sort of checklist and/or measurement system. I have found that mechanisms that prevent problems are cost effective and well worth the effort spent on designing them.

Sometimes when problems persist the causes are not so much a part of the details of the job or process, but are unrelated, obscure, and therefore often overlooked. One of the tools for getting to the root cause of a problem is to review a checklist of these obscure root causes. I have the following three on my checklist.

**1. Check what is being rewarded.** It is a truism that, "People will only do what they are rewarded to do." It may sound absurd, but what is being rewarded is sometimes the total opposite of the desired result. If you look around, you will be able to see examples of organizations that hope for the right behavior, but reward the wrong ones. Then they wonder why they fail at getting the desired results. Reward the right behavior and you will get the right results.

> *You don't get what you hope for, wish for, ask for, or beg for – you only get what you reward. Come what may, all living creatures will only do what is in there own best self-interest.*
>
> Michael LeBoeuf

For example, the board of directors wants top management to think long-term, but pays bonuses based on good profits and threatens job-security for poor profits. They then wonder why the CEO focuses on short-term profits rather than long-term business growth.

Michael LeBoeuf, a noted management consultant, teaches that one of the best examples of misalignment in reward systems is with customer service and frontline employees. A company hires them to treat customers well but rewards them based on something else. Most companies pay frontline employees a low flat hourly wage, provide little or no customer service training, and offer no special incentives. Then the company is surprised when its customers receive poor service.

Michael LeBoeuf says, "It is a rare company that has a well-planned reward system that meets the needs of employees as well as customers and stockholders. When you experience a company that provides consistent top quality service you can be assured that it is more than just luck in finding good employees."

If you are experiencing a persistent failure in your business or organization and you do not understand why people behave the way they do, ask the magic question – "What is being rewarded?" Whether it is planned or not, every organization has a reward system and sooner or later everyone figures out what it is and behaves the way the reward system teaches them to behave.

Rewards affect children in the same way. If you don't like the behavior of your children then ask yourself, "What am I rewarding?" Odds are you will discover, as I have, that the cause of a child's ill behavior is his or her own natural instinct to do what is being rewarded.

Change what you reward and your child's behavior will soon change. Children are very quick learners. I am surprised at how few parents seem to know about rewards. But now that you know it, you can act accordingly to improve your child's behavior. Remember that positive rewards work far better than negative ones.

**2. Check your objectives**, is next on the obscure root cause checklist. All good decisions are based on their ability to effectively produce the desired results, and the only way to know what is desired is to have thought out ahead of time what the appropriate objectives are for the situation at hand. Again it may sound absurd, but it is very often the case that the root cause of a persistent problem is that an objective is being used in the evaluation of a decision, but it is hidden and not being expressed.

> *To know what you want is to know what you will get; therefore, be certain of your desires.*
> Anonymous

You should be up-front and candid about objectives. Objectives are a critical element because you use them to determine your successes and failures. Therefore, you should not assume them. Make sure everyone's objectives have been expressed and make sure the final ones have been agreed to by all.

For example, as an engineer I have objectives that tend to focus on tangible and quantitative (cold fact) concerns. However, my wife Cathy has objectives that tend to focus more on the intangible and subjective (warm feeling) concerns. If we each express our objectives, we make a great team together and solve problems really well. However, when one of us does not express our objectives, it creates friction between us until we get all our objectives out on the table and at least acknowledge them. I find it helpful to write them out so there is no miscommunication.

The *Declaration of Independence* was essentially a written list of objectives. Some delegates to the Continental Congress wanted to include several other objectives that were very divisive at the time. Some of them are still controversial. Ben Franklin has been credited with the following saying; "Wisdom suggests that we fight only one battle at a time." The power of agreeing together on objectives can be seen by noting the countless men and women who have died to uphold those objectives.

It is important to identify all objectives because they also help determine what additional information is needed in order to make a good decision. Objectives help you to look beyond the apparent short-term alternatives and broaden your horizons. This is particularly true when objectives deal with your future happiness, because they can help you create long-term solutions that are more easily afforded in terms of time and money. As the saying goes, "short term pain gives you long term gain."

It is critical to success to clearly define objectives. Even if all objectives are known, they might not be defined well and may need adjustments. Sometimes objectives omit important considerations because they are too narrowly focused, either in time or in scope. Therefore you need to make sure your objectives are neither too brief nor too cursory.

Another key success factor when dealing with objectives is to focus on the "end" concerns, which are more fundamental to what you want to achieve, rather than relying too heavily on "means to the end" concerns. By identifying "end" objectives upfront, unbalanced decisions that cause failures are often avoided.

For example, I worked in the Marine Safety and Environmental Protection mission area of the Coast Guard. At times we focused our attention almost entirely on the "means to the end" objective of ensuring regulatory compliance. However, the more-important "end" concern – DON'T SPILL OIL – was often lost. When tanker designs changed, regulatory compliance actually got in the way of innovative piping system designs that would do a better job of preventing accidental oil spills. Fortunately for all citizens, the Coast Guard has seen the light and is now focusing on the "end" objective. Accidental oil spills have now declined to the point of almost being eliminated.

**3. Check your priorities** is last on my obscure root cause checklist. Two people may have the same priorities in life, but have two totally different lifestyles because they have ordered their priorities differently. I illustrate this with two fictitious men. The first one, let's call him Bob, has his priorities: family first, health second, and business third. If there is a conflict of resource allocation, such as time, the priorities make the choice. As a result of his priorities, Bob has a family who knows he is totally committed to them and they encourage him to work out at the gym. They support him in all of his business endeavors so he is very successful. He is truly a happy man.

> *The chief cause of failure and unhappiness is trading what you want most for what you want at the moment.*
> Robert Allen

The second man, Jim, has set his priorities as: business first, family second, and health third. Jim usually has enough money to meet obligations, but rarely vacations and spends little time outdoors or exercising; most would call him a workaholic. Jim's second wife spends much of her time transporting children to various programs and gets little assistance from Jim. Most of his business associates see him as being successful, but those who are closer to him do not see much happiness in his situation; they certainly don't envy him.

Organizations can mismanage their priorities in the same way. There was a company which had "Safety First" as a slogan but didn't live it as a priority. They put the slogan on everything, from mugs, to overalls, to calendars. However, what was well known by all of the employees that I came in contact with was that in reality, safety was a distant third behind expediency and profit. It was the kind of company that would spend a dollar to save a dime. The safety record showed the results; it was poor.

Another company that I am familiar with has similar operations, but a fantastic safety record. I believe it is doing well because the management has set priorities right and really puts "Safety First." Employees live the slogan that is displayed on their helmets. I do not think that it is a matter of luck that the real "Safety First" company is far more profitable than the other one.

> *Most people live in their own little world, but Einstein was great because he lived in a universe.*
> Deborah Gilbert

When you are searching for the root cause to a problem, persistence is the name of the game. Never give up. Keep on keeping on until you eventually find the root cause to the problem. A doctor once told me that the correct prognosis is 50% of the cure. Therefore, I believe it is reasonable to say that finding the right root cause to the problem is at least 50% of the solution.

Finding root causes to persistent problems is not an easy task; however, it can be made a lot easier if you go about it systematically. When you are in the mode of investigating what went wrong, make sure you keep your mind open. Let it expand out to focus on the periphery of the problem.

Always be in a learning mode, because technology is changing so fast that what was a correct answer yesterday might be the wrong answer today. By the *Law of Cause and Effect*, you can be assured that if you change a cause, you will alter the effect. Learn to eliminate the causes that keep you from achieving abundant life and you will make sure there is a rainbow after the rain.

✓ *Set up proactive detection methods that will quickly help to find root causes to problems and give you the opportunity to make adjustments to the process. Adopt the philosophy of learn and do, learn and do.*

✓ *It is important to use the right tool for the right job; therefore, fill your toolbox with tools that will help you detect the root causes to problems based on the situation.*

✓ *Check the more obscure root causes, such as: What is being rewarded? Have everyone's objectives been adequately defined and have all concerned agreed to them? Do you have the right priorities and are they set in the right order?*

# Strategy 5.

## *Overcome failures and solve problems like a genius.*

Hopefully you are realizing that failures are temporary and problems come in cycles. We are continuously being introduced to questions that need to be answered, decisions that need to be made, and problems that need to be solved. Richard feels unfulfilled in his job and questions whether he should look to find a new one. The major product in Sally's company is no longer profitable and she needs to decide whether to spend the money to improve it or to stop making it altogether. Harold and Susan just had another child, but now their house is not big enough; what should they do?

> *It's a good idea to learn from other people's experience, but usually with this caveat: seek out and learn from those with experience who are at the top of their game.*
>
> Dan Kennedy

I want to show you how to proactively answer questions, make decisions, and solve problems so that you have the highest likelihood of success. Being able to solve problems is not a matter of luck. Happy and successful people have fewer problems because they have learned how to solve them so that they either stay gone or are under control. It is time to stop solving problems like a gambler, hoping that the next pull on the crank of the one-armed bandit will be the winner. It is time to start solving problems like a genius.

I am not saying that problem solving is trivial, but rather the way you go about solving problems can be simplified by using the same systematic approach that has been used by the great geniuses of our time.

I remember well the admonishment from a boss of mine who became a mentor in the Coast Guard and later a partner in business; "Gilbert! – You work at headquarters … how do they address your mail? Isn't it 'Lieutenant Gilbert, Commandant?' Don't solve the problem like a Lieutenant, solve it like the Commandant!" I had been working on a project and looking at a marine safety problem from a very limited point of view. As a young Lieutenant, I felt powerless to do anything more than modify one little regulation. It might have made a small number of ships safer, but it would have cost the owners of other ships a lot of money unnecessarily.

My boss knew I could better solve the problem if I would look at it as if I had 30 years of experience and was empowered to solve the whole problem. I needed to "zoom out" so I could view the big picture and use all available resources.

It was good advice and I needed it. But how do you solve problems as if you have 30 years of experience when you are still "wet behind the ears?" How do you zoom out and expand your horizons and acquire the power to make more than little anemic fixes? How do you know which decision is the right one; so that everyone benefits? I began my quest for a proactive approach to problem solving.

**My problem solving quest** started by learning that it takes more than "thinking big" to solve problems efficiently and effectively. I have now spent several years studying various problem-solving methods, especially those used by some of the greatest geniuses of all time. People like Leonardo da Vinci, Albert Einstein, Thomas Edison, Benjamin Franklin, Andrew Carnegie, and Henry Ford. I believe these people became great because they all had used a systematic method for solving problems.

Based on my research, I have developed a hybrid proactive problem solving method. Following this proactive method has made a big difference in my professional and personal life. I have now been able to solve a lot of Coast Guard and other maritime business problems. Sometimes they seemed small and insignificant, and sometimes they had a huge impact in world shipping. I know from experience that this method works. I believe it will help you solve problems better than you ever have before.

The proactive problem solving method has *nine* distinct and necessary steps.  In order to remember them I have pegged them to the word – PROACTIVE.  The idea to use this word as an acronym came from a book called *Smart Choices – A Practical Guide to Making Better Decisions*, by John S. Hammond, Ralph L. Keeney, and Howard Raiffa.  Their book is excellent and I recommend it.  However, they only cover the decision-making part of problem solving; which is like putting all of the ingredients for an apple pie together, but not baking it.

> *Most worries are not half as serious as we first think they are.*
> Napoleon Hill

In the early 1980's I worked in New York City, next to Wall Street, with a co-worker who liked to follow the stock market.  He had lived in the city his entire life and was employed as a file clerk.  He would read the papers during his commute and keep up with the business activity of many companies.  Often he would remark to us how he had made the right choice about a company that was doing well.

One day I cautiously asked how much he made from the market.  The answer was an astounding – nothing.  He said he never actually purchased any stocks because he didn't want to take the chance of losing any money.  He feared making the wrong choice, so he never implemented his decisions and was no better off than if he hadn't made decisions at all.  He let himself be bound to mediocrity rather than SUCCESS BOUND.

I summarize the P R O A C T I V E steps below.  An example to illustrate the steps is provided after this explanation.  If you want to learn more, please look for my book, *Discover the Power of Proactive Thinking*, which will be printed next year.  (Visit my website http://www.RandyGilbert.com for previews.)

**Step 1. – Problem Statement**. Study the problem and write it out. The problem statement identifies and sets up boundaries around the problem so everyone involved can fully understand it. You develop the problem statement by asking questions, such as: What is the nature of the problem? When did it start? Who might be affected by it? How is the problem propagated? Where is it the worst? Why is it happening? Etc.

**Step 2. – Risk Assessment**. Research the problem thoroughly and assess the risks involved. Every problem has a certain level of risk and uncertainty associated with it. Analyze it to determine its seriousness; maybe it doesn't have to be solved at all. Next, make sure you know the root cause of the problem. Then, determine if it will bring harm and if so, how. Remove as much uncertainty about the problem as possible. This step is continuous and is especially necessary when the consequences of various alternative solutions are explored.

> *He who has no inclination to learn more will be very apt to think that he knows enough.*
>
>                                    Powell

**Step 3. – Objectives and Goals**. Identify and define all objectives and goals. Knowing the objectives of what is trying to be achieved is critical to knowing how best to solve the problem. It cannot be safely assumed that objectives and goals are already known or that everyone has the same ones. Fundamental ("end") objectives should be based on the major purpose of the individual or group involved; they are needed for evaluating alternatives, making decision tradeoffs, and choosing which performance measures are most appropriate. See Strategy 4 for more information on ensuring you have identified and defined all objectives.

**Step 4 – Alternative Solutions**. Develop all possible alternative solutions. An alternative course of action that meets one or more objectives represents one possible solution to a problem. This step needs to be separate from evaluating the consequences of the various alternatives because early assumptions or hasty conclusions might eliminate good alternatives too soon. A solution to a problem can be no better than the best alternative under consideration. Later on in Strategy 7, I discuss a "mind storming" tool that can be used to come up with hundreds of ideas for solutions.

**Step 5. – Consequence and Cost/Benefit Analyses.** You must explore how well each alternative would satisfy each stated objective. Identify the effectiveness, feasibility, costs, and benefits of each alternative under consideration. Look at all of the consequences (i.e. financial, legal, social, cultural, and moral implications) of a solution. I find it helpful to develop a matrix with alternatives listed down the first column and objectives across the top row.

**Step 6. – Tradeoffs and Decision-Making.** Begin the final decision making process by systematically comparing alternatives, two at a time. Review the consequences of each alternative and keep the dominant alternative, which is the one that best meets the objectives. Do this until one, or perhaps two, choices are left. If you have two that are equal, pick one and develop a solution, and hold the second as a backup. In his autobiography, Ben Franklin tells of how he used this type of system to make some of his more difficult choices in life.

Often you have two alternatives in which it is not clear which one is better, because they satisfy dissimilar objectives. It is like comparing apples and oranges. When this happens you need to employ an "equalizing tradeoff tactic" to make them comparable. This is usually done by finding a common denominator and then converting the objectives that are dissimilar to the common denominator. For example, I recently needed to get to Seattle for a conference. My airline flight choice came down to two alternatives, both costing the same and both leaving about the same time. However, one alternative flight had one stopover in Chicago, but was from an airline that I accumulated flight miles that are useable for free tickets. The second was a non-stop flight that would get me into Seattle 3 hours earlier, but I wouldn't get flight miles.  I converted the two objectives, flight miles and least amount of travel time, into dollars.  Since I could not earn any more money by getting to Seattle faster, the flight miles were worth more dollars, making the first alternative flight the best choice.  After making my decision I acted on it right away so the price of the ticket didn't change.

**Step 7. – Initial Action.**  After you've made a decision, take initial action right away.  Plan an implementation strategy, test it and improve it to maximize its viability and suitability.  The computer industry calls this "beta testing."  If you are not the one who will implement the solution, get the other person(s) involved to "try it out" in order to improve it and to validate that there are no hidden adverse consequences.

> *Experience never errs; it is only your judgment that errs in promising itself results as are not caused by your experiments.*
> Leonardo da Vinci

**Step 8. – Vigorous Deployment of the Implementation Strategy.** Vigorously deploy the solution.  Vigorous deployment is a firefighter's term.  Once the implementation plan has been developed and tested, don't waste any time; make it happen before circumstances change.  If other stakeholders are involved, coordinate efforts using good leadership, management, and communication tools.

**Step 9. – Evaluation of the Results.**  Set up performance measures based on the objectives and review the actions that have been taken to implement the solution.  Use the performance measures to see how effective the solution has been at reaching the stated objectives.  Also compare the costs and benefits experienced with those expected.  If one or more of your objectives are not satisfied, you start the PROACTIVE problem solving cycle again.  Because it is iterative, you can employ it again and again until the problem is solved or the situation is under control.

Good communication is a fundamental element that must be present in all steps of the PROACTIVE method.  You might say that it is the hub on which the rest of the wheel turns. An efficient flow of information needs to be communicated between yourself and all other persons involved throughout the entire process.

> *Failure is the mother of success.*
> Chinese Saying

This PROACTIVE method may sound a little complicated at first, because it has *nine* steps. However, it is quite simple and very useful once you learn it.

Let's look at an example problem. Vicki, a mother of four children and a teacher in a school, has an elderly mother who was going to require fulltime care, but Vicki didn't want to just put her mother in a nursing home. Vicki is an excellent teacher, has a real talent for working with children, and her family needed the second income. Vicki was not happy with her future prospects. She thought her only alternatives were to either quit her job and take care of her mother, or hire an in-home care provider. What should she do? What would you do?

In coming to me for help, I empathized with her and helped her to see that there are usually more options than one thinks. I then walked her through the PROACTIVE problem solving steps so that when she made her decision, she would be able to feel confident that she and her family were implementing the best solution. Here is how she applied the steps.

Starting with **P,** Vicki wrote out a problem statement so she knew what she was dealing with. She started out with "I need to find a way to take care of my mother." But with a little coaching, she realized that statement was too limiting and it put the burden on her alone. She "zoomed out" and began to see that the problem included at least two other aspects; satisfying the physical and emotional needs of her husband and children, and caring for her own physical and emotional needs. The problem statement became, "Our family needs to care for Grandma in such a way that her needs are met as well as ours."

Moving to step **R**, Vicki began reviewing the risk of the situation that she was facing. She asked herself and her family difficult questions and tried to be as realistic with them as possible. Questions such as: "How long is Grandma expected to live? Is there anything that we do not want to expose our children to? Does Grandma need professional medical care that can't be provided at home? Would we feel bad if Grandma was in a nursing home? Would the children benefit from having Grandma at home? Would plans to get the family farm going again be set back further?"

Vicki learned from her research that her family wanted to help care for Grandma and that with a little bit of training they could all provide Grandma the care she needed. She also learned from the doctor that Grandma could live for several more years and, given the right positive therapy her health, could improve. Vicki and her husband both agreed that their children would mature from exposure to a death situation should it occur, and also that they wanted their children to grow up to be compassionate, and helping Grandma would assist with that.

Next came **O**, identify objectives. After researching the problem, Vicki began writing down the objectives of what she and her family wanted to happen. She asked her husband and children "how would you describe the best situation?" She found it more difficult to describe her own, but she finally came up with the following objectives.

1. Grandma is happy, safe, and well cared for.
2. The family has sufficient income to meet all expenses.
3. The children get quality time from mom and dad.
4. The children get to spend meaningful time with grandma.
5. The family continues plans for starting the family farm.
6. Vicki continues to work with children.
7. Vicki starts a business.

In the process of doing the first 3 steps (**P, R,** and **O**), it became evident that there could be opportunities to actually make the situation better than it was. Vicki had always wanted to start her

> *A genius is simply one who has taken full possession of his own mind and directed it toward objectives of his own choosing, without permitting out-side influences to discourage or mislead him.*
>
> Napoleon Hill

own business, but she thought that those plans would have to wait until her children were grown and gone. By listing the 7th objective the way she did, Vicki was taking a bold step in the direction of doing what she felt she was always meant to do.

Next came the **A** step, so Vicki started listing possible alternatives. She and her family came up with four that they considered.

- A. Vicki continues to teach and family hires a daycare provider for grandma.
- B. Vicki quits her job and cares for grandma full time at home.
- C. Vicki gets a different part-time job and hires a part-time care provider.
- D. Vicki starts a family business at home; whole family cares for grandma.

For step **C**, Vicki began analyzing the consequences of each alternative by judging how well each of them met her stated objectives. She created a matrix, like the one below, which helped her see how each alternative compared to the others. She used a 1-2-3 numbering scale to signify how well each objective would be satisfied; 1 meaning little to none, 2 meaning about half-half; and 3 meaning most to all.

| Objectives<br>Alternatives | 1 | 2 | 3 | 4 | 5 | 6 | 7 |
|:---:|:---:|:---:|:---:|:---:|:---:|:---:|:---:|
| **A** | 2 | 3 | 2 | 1 | 1 | 3 | 1 |
| **B** | 3 | 2 | 3 | 3 | 3 | 1 | 1 |
| **C** | 2 | 2 | 2 | 2 | 2 | 1 | 1 |
| **D** | 3 | 2 | 3 | 3 | 3 | 3 | 3 |

> *Experience teaches us that we can always find a solution to a problem if we take the time to analyze the situation and develop an appropriate response.*
> Anonymous

Next came **T**, the trade-off and decision making step. Vicki started by looking for alternatives that could be paired together where one of them was clearly better than the other. She noticed that when **B** and **C** were paired, **B** had equal or higher ratings than **C**, so she eliminated **C**. Next she paired **B** and **D**; **D** had equal or higher ratings, so she eliminated **B**. That left only **A** and **D**, which had dissimilar consequences.

Since the rating for objective **1** was higher for alternative **A** than **D**, Vicki decided to use an equalizing tradeoff tactic on objectives **1** and **2**, because she felt that she could convert them both to the common denominator of money. Objective **1** was easy to convert because it started out as a dollar comparison. However, objective **2** was converted by thinking of what it would "cost" the family in worry, and then multiplying the ratings given for each alternative. After Vicki converted them both to dollars, she added the dollars in objectives **1** and **2** together. The alternative **D** total value came out to be $5,000 more annually than alternative **A**, which meant alternative **D** was clearly the best. So **D,** "Starting a family farm business with flexible hours and moving Grandma in to live with the family" was their decision.

Vicki was very relieved at having made the decision. One of the best things about this PROACTIVE method for solving problems is that you can feel confident in the decision that has been made. Plus, you can explain with ease and clarity to others why you made the choice you did. Also, if new information is brought up, or if your situation changes, it is easy to see where adjustments can be made and it becomes easier to modify the solution and be flexible.

Since Vicki has a contract with the school to teach to the end of the school year, she is still in the **I** step; taking initial action and developing her implementation plan. Vicki and her family took some classes together from a local adult home. Her husband installed a wheel chair ramp and modified one of the bathrooms to add handicap amenities. Grandma has moved in and Vicki hired someone to care for her during the daytime. Vicki is also preparing a complete business plan for the family farm and a riding school for children. Grandma's health is already showing signs of improvement.

Vicki is very enthusiastic about the future. When the school year is over, she will be ready to do the **V** step and vigorously deploy the solution. She will let the school board know she is leaving and will begin working on her new business over the summer. For step **E**, Vicki has planned family meetings to review how well things are going. She has put each of her children in charge of overseeing certain parts of the implementation plan and they will make a report to the family with recommendations for improvement.

Vicki and her family are fortunate. They have taken proactive steps to solving their problem. Some people however, tend to look at problems from a negative point of view. Even if something hasn't gone wrong yet, they worry about the future. Worry can be a killer. It only places additional burdens on you and doesn't help. In his famous *Sermon on the Mount* speech, Jesus warned, "Do not worry about tomorrow for tomorrow will worry about itself; today has enough troubles of its own."

> *Worry is like a rocking chair. It keeps you busy, but it doesn't get you anywhere.*
> Will Rogers

It is far better to approach life in a constructive proactive way. When a potential problem situation approaches I try to develop possible alternative solutions. Then I decide which alternative "future" would be the best and try to work toward that future. When you carefully plan responses to every possible problem, you won't have to spend your time in unnecessary worry.

Sometimes failures and problems come suddenly and you do not have a lot of time to analyze the situation before a decision needs to be made and action taken. In such cases, don't get stuck with paralysis by analysis.   Make decisions and act as quickly as possible.   Be aware of priorities and protect your most valuable resources.   For example, if you get cut, stop the bleeding first, and then figure out what to do next.   It is always best to do emergency response planning when the risk to people or the environment is high.   Children practice fire drills at school, and hopefully at home, so they know what to do if that unwanted disaster strikes.   Fire drills should be carried out whenever large numbers of people work in buildings, especially old ones.   This is a proactive way to approach potential problems and it helps emergency personnel solve problems ahead of time.

Airline pilots spend hours in simulators practicing appropriate responses to all foreseeable failures and problems.   Sports teams drill over and over again, practicing plays that will give the best position to defend a goal or score against their opponent. Negotiating teams develop points and responses to every possible gambit that might be used by the other side.   Generals spend days, weeks, and months thinking through every possible move that might be made by the enemy in battle.   These are all proactive ways of solving problems ahead of time and preparing for the future.   These types of drills protect us against unnecessary worry, save lives, and bring us ultimate success and victory in life.

> *People don't become successful by always making the right decisions, but because they always make decisions in the right way.*
> Brian Tracy

After the rush of a problem is over, make sure you take the time to learn from the situation and make necessary corrections.   When a fire breaks out on a ship, the first response is to contain it and put it out.    Then the Captain and his crew figure out what happened and how they will keep it from happening again.

Fires on ships are more common than the general public is aware of.   It is a constant problem solving experience.   Ship's crews regularly conduct drills so they know what to do when a fire breaks out.   However, I believe they should also regularly use the

PROACTIVE method so their problem solving will be more effective, resulting in fewer fires.

By using the PROACTIVE method you will break free from mediocrity because you will be solving problems like a genius. As you deal with each problem you will notice that your worry and stress will diminish and you will become a much happier person. Being proactive and looking toward the future is always better than being reactive and dwelling on the past.

Although I am involved in many more businesses, activities, and organizations than the average person, I feel that I can have an abundant life that is filled with peace, because I am able to rid myself of problems quickly. When I lived in Hawaii I experienced more rainbows than I could ever count. Sometimes I would see double and even triple rainbows with spectacular colors. I guarantee you, that by learning to systematically solve problems like a genius, your life will become like an island paradise and nature will ensure your rainbows come out after the rain.

✓ *By using the PROACTIVE problem solving method you will be able to think and act like a genius. You will have less stress and worry, which equates to an abundant life.*

✓ *When you are in a potentially harmful situation, think ahead about what you will do if a problem should arise. Emergency response planning must be done ahead of time.*

*"If you have an important point to make, don't try to be subtle or clever.  Use a pile driver.  Hit the point once.  Then come back and hit it again. Then hit it a third time – a tremendous whack."*

Sir Winston Churchill

# Part II

# Wisdom for Young and Old

*Everything is changing so fast that we can't stop learning; everyone needs wisdom, no matter how old you are. Since this new anti-gravity scooter could be dangerous, I need to learn how to fly it safely just as much as you do.*

## Foreword to Part II

King Solomon, the third king of the Israelites, is known to be the wisest (and richest) ever to have lived. It is said that God had asked him what he would like to have and his reply was that he wanted to have wisdom. Solomon's request pleased God so much that he gave him the wisdom he asked for, and because his request was so unselfish, God said He would bless him with riches too.

In the Bible, Saint James says, "if anyone lacks wisdom let him ask of God, who gives it freely to all people who ask." If we too are given the promise of wisdom, the question that must be asked is, "how did God give Solomon wisdom and is it the same for us?"

If one reads the books written by Solomon, it becomes obvious that he received his wisdom by reflecting on life. Solomon became an extremely careful observer of what went on around him. One important thing to note is that Solomon seemed to pay as much attention to the failures of people as anything else. I believe we can do the same with the same result.

In my studies as to how we learn and ultimately gain wisdom, I've come to see that the entire learning process is systematic. We gather data over time and integrate it into information, which we then collate from many areas and further integrate it into knowledge. The knowledge that we continue to gain from skills and life's experiences is integrated into understanding.

There remains the last critical step, because understanding by itself is not wisdom, it is only the ability to control. In order to have wisdom you must be able to give direction to control and point your life toward what is good and right. You must reflect on life.

The strategies of Part II clearly show you how to turn the failures and adversities of life into wisdom. You can have wisdom at any age; you need not be old and gray. As you grow in wisdom and implement the strategies of this book, I hope you will answer this question for yourself. "Did Solomon's success and abundance come as a direct result of having extraordinary wisdom?"

# *Strategy 6.*

# *Let failure be your teacher of wisdom.*

Sooner or later the person who is serious about succeeding in life – the person who wants to be free of mediocrity – must ask the following questions: "Where does wisdom come from?" and "How do I get it?" Success demands wisdom. Without attaining wisdom, people only have a limited level of understanding about how things function. Understanding is not enough. You need to have a higher understanding of how things function so you can control them <u>and</u> you need to know how to choose the right thing to do with your control. That only comes from wisdom.

> *Consider it pure joy, my brothers, whenever you face trials of many kinds, because you know that the testing of your faith develops perseverance. Perseverance must finish its work so that you may be mature and complete, not lacking anything.*
>
> Saint James

Let me give an example from my teen years of the danger of having understanding without wisdom. At an early age, I was taught most everything I needed to know about cars and engines as I helped my father fix and maintain them. You might say that I had a good <u>knowledge</u> about how cars worked. When I was age 10, I received a go-cart for Christmas and began to learn how to drive. At age 12, I was allowed to drive our old 1942 Willy's Army jeep around. At this point I was gaining an <u>understanding</u> of how cars operated and how to control them. I received my license at age 14 and began driving to school. I was a fearless teen behind a wheel, which is dangerous at best.

At age 14 (the legal driving age back then) I had convinced the authorities that my understanding of how to operate a car was sufficient for a license; however, I had not yet obtained much <u>wisdom</u> about the safe way to operate a car – I had understanding without control. I drove too fast and was a bit of a show-off. In less than a year I had a serious accident. I had been driving too fast. Fortunately, the only injury was my pride.

I believe that wisdom does come from failures and that was a big one for me. I lost the use of the car, which was totaled in the crash. I also lost my license for the next several months. The wise judge pointed out that it would give me enough time to learn the wisdom that I had previously lacked.

I also had a very strong incentive to learn my lesson because I had my sights set on being accepted into one of the military academies. The academies are looking for leaders who can learn from mistakes, and another accident would prove I couldn't.

You might say that failure became my teacher of wisdom. Just experiencing a car crash does not mean you've acquired wisdom; because there were other teens I knew who had had similar experiences, yet some of them didn't seem to have gained any wisdom. They continued to drive just as dangerously afterwards. What makes the difference?

One of the differences I believe is that some people do not understand where wisdom comes from. It is more than experience; it is reflection on experience. Wisdom comes from matching experience up against the universal laws of nature. For example, I believe God gave the world the *Law of Sowing and Reaping* so we could learn wisdom from it.

The *Law of Sowing and Reaping* teaches the farmer that if he plants a certain type of seed, then he can be assured that he will reap a crop of that same type of seed. The farmer is able to turn the understanding of planting into wisdom as he learns by experience the best time of the year to plant and the best time to harvest in order to maximize his yield. He might also learn how crop rotation or certain types of fertilizers can help. The wise farmer observes and learns from mistakes and problems. America is blessed with a lot of wise farmers.

> *Sometimes a noble failure serves the world as faithfully as a distinguished success.*
> Dowden

The *Law of Sowing and Reaping* also applies to the mental realm and therefore we can learn things like self-control. If we are allowed to "pay for our mistakes" then we learn how to change our thoughts and behaviors. It applies both positively and negatively. If you work hard, you will reap an advancing career. If you don't push yourself, then you reap being stuck at a level that will be unfulfilling. If you make more calls, you will inevitably reap more sales. If you are not careful with spending, you will reap financial troubles.

Drs. Cloud and Townsend point out in their book, *Boundaries With Kids*, "The *Law of Sowing and Reaping* gives us a healthy fear … a healthy respect for consequences keeps us living in reality and moving in a good direction." Cloud and Towsend point out the importance of teaching children how to learn from their mistakes, because if children don't learn, they lose out on both the positive and negative sides. We must learn from failures so that we can be motivated to do good work and at the same time to fear irresponsibility and other character problems.

Finally, the *Law of Sowing and Reaping* applies to the spiritual world, which gives us the ability to have happiness, joy, and peace of mind. Saint Paul said it this way, "A man reaps what he sows. The one who sows to please his sinful nature, from that nature will reap destruction; the one who sows to please the Spirit, from the Spirit will reap eternal life." Our entire lives are spent learning to defeat our sinful nature and the wisdom needed comes from God Himself. I will talk more about this in the bonus strategy.

One thing is for certain; if you are not willing to learn from your failures, then wisdom will elude you, and the seeds of greatness are not in you. You are condemning yourself to experiencing that same problem over and over again. If you want to be SUCCESS BOUND, you need to have an open mind and quickly admit when you have a problem. Next, you need to do something different so that the problem won't reoccur.

Some teachers of success have suggested that the word *failure* be struck from our vocabulary. I respectfully disagree. Wisdom comes from reflecting on our trial and error experiences. I believe that what is meant by such advice is that no one <u>is a failure</u>. The only people that might come close to being labeled failures are the ones who refuse to learn from their experiences, usually because they have given up on themselves

> *Failure is, in a sense, the highway to success, inasmuch as every discovery of what is false leads us to seek earnestly after what is true, and every fresh experience points out some form of error, which we shall afterward carefully avoid.*
>
> Keats

I believe that it is the word *impossible* that should be struck from our vocabulary. During his study of over 500 successful men and women, Napoleon Hill discovered that they acknowledged and welcomed failure, defeat, adversity, etc., but they never let the word *impossible* into their vocabulary. The key to managing failure is to quickly acknowledge its presences and then remove its cloak of disguise so the true identity, which is opportunity, is revealed.

The Bible teaches that "nothing is impossible to them who believe" and it confirms that failures and struggles will come our way if we love God. I believe our failures become our "rainbow signs." We need the rain to have the rainbow.

We will naturally make mistakes and learn from them and the promise remains solid, that never again will God seek to destroy us. In fact, the opposite is true. He has made every means available for us to learn how to love and serve our fellow man. The Bible tells us that God has put His own Spirit within believers and has given us the gifts of knowledge and wisdom.

The acquiring of wisdom can be enhanced by adversity. Problems create a strong need to learn quickly about a situation. You can be proactive. Use every result that doesn't meet your expectations to speed your learning process along.  It is like sailing against the wind.  The stronger the wind, the easier it is to use, but the more skill will be required to control the sailboat.  When adversity comes, take advantage of the heightened desire and use the higher energy level to learn what you need to know in order to solve the problem in the right way.

Be proactive and think ahead about what you need to learn so that when the opportunity presents itself, you will be ready.  When I am in a situation of adversity, I ask myself, 'What one thing can I learn now that will help me the most?'  Then I focus on that one thing.  This is particularly helpful when learning that one thing leads directly to learning the next.

> *The man who never made a mistake, never did anything. ... very little comes out right the first time. Failures, repeated failures, are fingerprints on the road to achievement.*
> John C. Maxwell

I have found that setting stretch goals increases my chance of failure, particularly when I set hard-to-meet deadlines.  I have found that my subconscious mind will go to work trying to figure out how to arrange all the tasks that need to be accomplished and all of the resources that need to be gathered and used.  This includes the knowledge and organizational skills I need in order to meet that deadline.

One nice thing about a self-imposed deadline is that you can regulate your rate of failure.  When I miss a self-imposed deadline it is a pseudo-failure that helps me to continuously improve my efficiency in getting things done.  It causes me to ask myself, 'How can I be faster?'

I have found that it is better to set mini-goals that are performance-oriented, which I can control and reward myself for, rather than setting major goals that may be influenced by others or require perfection before reward.  I figure that improving the little things will have a consistent positive effect on improving the big things.

I have also found that seeking wisdom by reflecting on failures is like praying and asking God for something. Sometimes I don't ask in the right way, so I don't learn the lesson well. Jesus said, "ask and you shall receive, that your joy may be made full." God wants us to learn wisdom. He wants to give it to us, but how do we ask for wisdom?

**Asking for wisdom.**

Tony Robbins says, "When you ask, you must ask intelligently, that means you need to ask the right person and in the right way." Tony teaches not to ask for a million dollars from someone who doesn't earn more than $30,000 per year. What good would that do? Ask for something from someone who you know has what you want.

I believe the same goes for wisdom. If you want to learn wisdom about raising children, don't ask the bachelor who was an only child. If you want to learn wisdom about how to recognize the love of your life, then don't ask your friend who has been divorced twice.

Jesus also added a little caveat when he said, "Ask for anything in My name and it shall be given to you." I don't think that Jesus was just giving us some magic words to utter, "In Jesus' Name." I believe He was telling us that we should ask for what He wants us to have so we can fulfill our purpose in life. As it relates to wisdom, it means we need to be in alignment with the "BIG picture." We need to live by the universal laws that He established for the world so we can do a good job. It means you should ask for wisdom in all of the areas that matter to your success in fulfilling your purpose.

For example, I am in business and if there is a contract that I really want, then there are specific things I must do in preparation. I have to make sure that I know what the critical success factors are and then plan to satisfy each one. My success will be limited to my ability regarding the weakest one – just like the weak link of a chain. My past failures have helped me to discover which critical success factors need to be improved. I am asking for wisdom to improve these.

> *Temporary setbacks become learning experiences that prepare you for success when it eventually arrives.*
> W. Clement Stone

Every once in while I talk to someone who has just gone through a major upset or failure. When I ask, 'if you had a choice, would you do the same thing again?' I am always amazed when they reply "Absolutely." Some say that without the upset they might still be working at some dead-end job, or that they would not have known this other person who now means so much to them. If that is going to be your response then you are on the right track – you are on the fast track to wisdom.

You will not learn wisdom if you get angry and frustrated because of failures. I recommend you build up a proactive attitude toward them. Try to develop a way to celebrate when you learn a lesson from a mistake or failure. It might be the turning point in your life that brings you success. Not acknowledging failures will leave you chained to mediocrity like a slave. Choose freedom now – it is yours for the taking.

You are the one who chooses whether or not to remain tied to mediocrity. Deciding to embrace the learning process will loosen the bonds. If you sell yourself short on your efforts to learn, then you are missing a significant aspect of your life. There is no personal improvement without the intentional effort to learn wisdom. Don't be left behind while the rest of us move along toward greater prosperity and peace of mind. Make up your mind to reflect on your experiences and to learn the wisdom that is born of adversity – let failures be your teacher of wisdom.

✓ *Learn from your failures, then you will have more than just an experience. Reflection will let your inner wisdom teach you right from wrong.*

✓ *Learning about universal laws and setting stretch goals will help you to acquire wisdom at a more rapid rate.*

✓ *You should seek out wisdom in a proactive way.*

# Strategy 7.

## Overcome failures systematically.

Have you ever played the game called "Memory?"  You spread out a deck of cards face down.  Each player turns over two cards at a time, trying to find pairs.  If they don't match then they are returned face down.  One or two turns later when you want to find the same card, you realize that your memory has blurred the original card with its neighbors and you can't tell them apart.

What went wrong?  You catalogued the first mismatched pair as a failure and moved on with your life.  But this is not enough.  You have to learn from the failures or you will repeat them.  When you take the time to learn their lessons then they will also clue you in as to where your successful matches lie.  Set up a system for failing in which failure is not only an acceptable option, but so that you will learn as much as possible with each try.  It's called "learn and do, learn and do, learn and do."

> *Every failure is a step to success; every detection of what is false directs us toward what is true; every trial exhausts some tempting form of error.  Not only so, but scarcely any attempt is entirely a failure; scarcely any theory, the result of steady thought, is altogether false; no tempting form of error is without some latent charm derived from truth.*
> **Whewell**

Thomas Edison set up a systematic method of eliminating all of the ways that he couldn't invent the light bulb.  In order to explain his system to a group of young students, predominantly from Latin America, I told them to imagine that Edison had a huge bag of beans (frijoles) – thousands of them.  To Edison, each bean represented one of his ideas which might make a light bulb.  He was confident that at least one of those beans was the right one.  His job was then finding at least one idea bean that worked.  He remained confident, even after many tries, because he knew for certain that at least one of his ideas would do the trick, if he could only find which one.  Edison holds the record on the number of U.S. patents because he learned how to fail systematically.

Thomas Edison set up a way of systematically taking each idea bean out of his bag, one at a time, and examining it to see if it was the idea that would light up the room.  When he got up to experiment 9,999, he was asked by a reporter, "Sir are you going to fail 10,000 times?"  He confidently replied that he did not fail at each attempt; rather he succeeded at discovering another idea that would not work.  He never gave up because he still had plenty of idea beans in his bag and a systematic way of checking each one.

Too many times we give up because we don't have any beans left in our bag.  Our problem is that we usually start off with too few idea beans in our bag.  Here is an exercise that I learned in order to increase the number of idea beans in my bag.  I learned it years ago from Brian Tracy, one of the most gifted teachers I have ever had.  My experience is the same as his.  No one who has used this exercise to come up with ideas has been disappointed.  If you use it, you are guaranteed to come up with more ideas than you have ever thought possible.  You will have a head full of ideas, which will give you the persistence of Thomas Edison.

The exercise is called **mindstorming**.  It is similar to group *brainstorming*, but you perform it alone.  It goes like this.  Take a piece of paper and write at the top of it a pressing problem or a question of deep concern.  Then number the lines 1 through 20.  Write on each line one way of how you might solve the problem or answer the question.  The first ten or so will come fairly quickly and seem obvious, just put them down.  You will begin to experience more difficultly as you work on the last 5 to 7.

Do not judge your solutions yet, just let your imagination take over and write down every idea that comes to mind.  Sometimes it is beneficial to think "out of the box," so give yourself permission to write down (now stay with me here) ludicrous, illegal, or even immoral ideas.  Remember, it is important not to judge the ideas while you are writing them.  When you've completed writing all

20, go back down the list and bring the illegal and immoral ideas back "into the box" by converting the essence of the ideas into an appropriate context. For example, if you were in a retail business and needed to increase sales, one immoral solution might be to have your customer service people come to work naked. The essence of the idea is "there is nothing to hide". Therefore, you would instruct your customer service people to be completely honest about everything, even the negative aspects your products.

> *A healthy hunger for a great idea is the beauty and blessedness of life.*
> Jean Ingelow

Sometimes it is difficult to write specific solutions because images and pictures come to your mind. That is OK, because that is how our minds think best – with pictures. Just describe or draw the pictures as your mind sees them. Albert Einstein came up with the theory of relativity when he saw a picture in his mind of himself riding a wave of light through the universe.

Do this type of exercise regularly and your head will be swimming with ideas. To make use of your ideas, choose those that seem to have the highest likelihood of solving your problem. I've found it very useful to start with a clean piece of paper and write each idea as a problem statement in the form of a question, 'How would I put that particular idea into practice.' It is amazing to see how many ideas mindstorming can generate.

There are some variations to mindstorming that I have found useful. One is to write the problem in a couple of different ways and do the mindstorming exercise for each way. This really helps me to look at the situation from different points of view. For example, sometimes I pretend I am a different person and try to take on that other person's character and style of thinking.

One of my favorite ways of modifying the process is to think of 20 ways to make the problem or situation worse. Try this some time. It might help; especially if you are in little bit of a negative mood. When using it on one particularly highly emotional problem that I had, it actually made me start to laugh because I thought of some pretty crazy ways to make things worse.  When you are doing this type of backwards mindstorming, review your list and either write down the opposite action, or think of what you would do to prevent that bad thing from ever really happening.  You will be surprised at how creative it can help you to become.

> By what strange law of mind is it that an idea long overlooked and trodden under foot as a useless stone, suddenly sparkles out in new light as a discovered diamond?
>
> Mrs. Stowe

When you have a very bag full of idea beans to use, you will never get discouraged, even when you have a solution that doesn't work out.  Look at the situation in the way that Thomas Edison did and congratulate yourself for finding another way that didn't work.  Learn from the mistake, laugh as you throw the bean out, and reach into your bag for another idea.

I have discovered that when I become more aware of what I can do to overcome my failures, I gain courage and tenacity.  If you want to develop the ability to keep going, even after you have repeatedly failed at every attempt, then you must do the same.  It is almost as if nature is saying "how bad do you really want it?"  When you create within yourself a burning desire to accomplish your major purpose in life, you will gain an attitude of persistence that will overcome any obstacle.  Such persistence will ensure that you systematically gain sound wisdom from your failures.

✓ *Use solution generating methods like mindstorming and fill your mind with countless ideas.  Your mind is an unlimited resource.  Consider that there are many ways of making light.*

✓ *Get in the habit of asking yourself for more ideas, regardless of whether or not you ever use them.  You're not in control if you have only one possible solution; always have lots of them.*

✓ *Get organized.  Eliminate the ideas that won't work.  With the remaining ideas, consider the possibility that some might work better if combined; then figure out which ideas you could match for a winning combination.*

# Strategy 8.

# Learn from other people's failures.

We live during a time when we must carefully consider how to manage our resources. One of the resources that I consider to be important is our time resource. Time is not renewable. You cannot save time. We are all given the same amount and it is ticking away for all of us at the same rate. What you must do in order to manage your resources properly is to learn how to manage time. You must make the most out of it.

> *The number one key to success is to learn from the experts.*
> Brian Tracy

One of the most effective ways to make the best use of our time is to optimize our learning time. And the absolute best way to optimize our time is to learn from the experts, those who have suffered the failures and have spent weeks, months, and years reading, experimenting, and learning all there is to know in a particular field. These people become our role models and mentors.

We also have the ability to learn from our anti-role models. Such people make mistake after mistake and are the type that you would never want to emulate. It does no good to get mad at them or to try to change them, but rather learn from their mistakes. Surprisingly, some people are both kinds of people. I am convinced that my father can build or fix anything. He is a genius when it comes to mechanical abilities. But, he divorced my mother when I was in high school and is now married to his fourth wife. Fortunately I picked up his natural talent for building things (I built my entire home and I can fix or repair just about anything). However, I have also learned by his mistakes regarding women. I strive to continuously "fix" anything that would interfere with maintaining a loving relationship with my wife.

Thomas Edison invented one kind of light bulb. There are now hundreds of different types of bulbs, tubes, gadgets, and gizmos that produce light. I recently saw an advertisement for customized lighting for office buildings. I was truly amazed at what seemed like an endless variety. Do you think the inventors of all those lights started from scratch? Of course not. They learned from Thomas Edison and other inventors so they didn't need to make the same mistakes. They advanced the designs of lights further because they figuratively stood on the shoulders of other industry giants.

After learning from others, they expanded the knowledge of making lights and applied it in new directions. You must do the same. Read and observe what others have done so that you don't need to cover the same ground.

Due to a poor business decision a while back (a 'failure') I learned a tremendous lesson and I am now able to make better decisions. I needed to invest thousands of dollars on legal counsel. I learned to look on the positive side and trusted that it was all for my own good. Not more than a year later I received the real payback from that bit of adversity. I learned something of greater value than money. Upon reflection, I realized that <u>lawyers get paid a lot of money for helping others, because they know all about the man-made laws that govern businesses</u>. It sounds simple, but this was my seed of opportunity that came out of adversity! Read on to find out why.

Putting two and two together, I discovered that if I want to be able to help people to solve problems and become more successful in a proactive way, then I needed to become someone who knows all about the universal laws that govern peoples lives and businesses. Since the universal laws govern our mental, spiritual and physical world, knowing how to apply them will turn failures into successes.

It seemed a simple concept, but who could teach me to become an expert of universal laws? I began looking around to find the giants, those who would carry me upon their shoulders. I had already been studying how people could use the principles of proactive thinking to optimize their business performance and solve problems. I knew that these areas would be related and would expand into the study of how we could improve our lives so that we could enjoy peace of mind and abundance. I discovered that the people who had become successful at managing the failures of their lives were those giants. Those men and women painstakingly learned the universal laws and used them as their strategies for success. I was excited!

> *The way of a fool is right in his own eyes, but a wise man listens to counsel. ... Listen to counsel and accept discipline, that you may be wise all of your life.*
> King Solomon

I began reviewing all of the resources I could get my hands on. I did searches on the Internet, at libraries and bookstores. I searched my Bible and studied the great philosophers. I began adding a whole new section to my personal library. No single source taught universal laws. However, collectively I was finding what I needed. It was like gathering the "success giants" together as a team. Each had mastered different aspects of how to manage failure, adversity, and defeat, and turned them into seeds of greater opportunity for success.

It makes sense that, if we learn about and then follow all of the universal laws of the natural, mental, and spiritual worlds that are related to managing our failures, we can enjoy a relatively rapid learning curve. I see it as getting onto the "fast track to wisdom." You don't have to be old and gray to be wise. It is all about developing learning into a strategy. Do this and you will avoid years of trial and error. I mention a few laws in this strategy, but other universal laws are scattered throughout the book where they are most appropriate.

The *Law of Cause and Effect* is one of the most important laws associated with managing failures, because it is the foundation of so many others. Simply stated, it means that for every effect you see in this world there is a definite cause. In 425 BC, the Greek philosopher Socrates, postulated it as the *Law of Causality*. He said, "We live in a world of law, governed by a system of order, whether we understand the principles behind them or not." He caused people to logically think through the consequences of their thoughts and actions. This law works both ways. You can either use it to plan your actions (causes), to achieve certain results (effects), or you can observe an effect and then backtrack to find out what caused it.

While in the Coast Guard I was involved in investigations of marine casualties; most were ships that had capsized and sunk. Our accident investigations were similar to the highly publicized ones conducted by the FAA for airplane accidents. The primary purpose for spending so much money on accident investigations is so a determination can be made as to the exact cause of the accident.

By the *Law of Cause and Effect*, we knew that if we could prevent the causes from happening in the future, that we would, given the same circumstance, prevent the accident (the effect). I saw over and over again that when the primary cause was preventable, it had a definite lowering of the accident rate. This law is dependable; you bet your life on it every time you fly a jetliner or sail on a cruise ship.

> *Worrying about the future is NOT preparation for it – never has been – never will be. If you worry about the future, then worry about your happiness, because it is in jeopardy.*
>
> Unknown

I've also learned that this law covers the mental world as well as the physical. It is a simple truth that thought precedes all actions. It means that, if you control your thoughts, you will control your actions. Since certain types of thoughts (causes), produce certain types of actions (effects), you can be responsible for the part of the world that you control.

Since the Creator has given us complete control over our thoughts, it follows that He wants us to use our thoughts to obtain the things He wants us to have. Of course this law may not readily apply if what you are trying to achieve is selfishly motivated or at odds with nature.

If you combine the above link between thought and action with the fact that there is no limit to the amount that you can improve your mind, then you are without limit in anything that you can eventually do, be or have. NO LIMIT! As Brian Tracy says, "you can learn anything you need to learn to achieve any goal that you set for yourself" The reason is because of the *Law of Cause and Effect*. This is important because if you find that someone is having the kind of success you want, all you have to do is think the same type of thoughts they are thinking, do the same type of things that they are doing and you will receive the same types of successful results. There is no other way – it's a universal law and nature will not violate itself.

The *Law of Attraction* is another law that is important to understand. The *Law of Attraction* says that in the mental world, like will attract like. It is no surprise that people who think and talk about what they want, have the things they want. If you think positive thoughts then you will attract into your life other good people who think positive thoughts. If you are always sure that circumstances will work out to your benefit then you will eventually attract the right circumstances.

> *Struggle is a clever device through which nature compels humanity to develop, expand and progress. It is either an ordeal or a magnificent experience, depending on one's attitude toward it. Success is impossible – unthinkable even – without it.*
> Napoleon Hill

Unfortunately for some the law works in the opposite direction too. The people who think and talk about (i.e., complain about) the things they don't want always seem to attract into their lives more of the things they don't like. Since this is a universal law there is no other way, complainers and whiners will always get more of what they don't want. If and when they get tired of thinking and complaining about bad things then their fortune will turn around.

Sometimes opportunity comes disguised as failure or adversity. It doesn't look like something that would help you attain your goal, but <u>don't be fooled!</u> You must always remember that, if you have been thinking and talking about what you want, then the failure or adversity must be viewed as a gift – one that is wrapped up in a problem. If you throw this gift out or ignore it, you will have missed something that may cut years off the time it takes you to achieve your goal.

I have heard people tell how they lost a job or a major contract, only to find out later that it was exactly what they needed so they would move in a different direction.

In the movie *Forrest Gump,* Forrest spoke the words, "… it happens," which renewed a similar phrase well used by persons chained to mediocrity. Such persons see their circumstances as random parts of life, which are simply meant to be endured. They refuse to see that their actions have an effect one way or another. Such persons are doomed to have the same lesson repeat itself until they, by chance, learn it. I've met several bitter people that never learned the lessons they were meant to learn. Instead of a life that could have been filled with triumph and success, they can only recall with bitterness all of the bad things God had forced them to endure.

In writing this, I am thinking of one person in particular. She has lived in unhappiness for almost her entire life. It is an awful shame, because she has tremendous artistic talent. From what I have seen of her work, I would consider her talent to be on par with the greatest. However, her enjoyment of her talent is limited by a very low self-esteem; it has been her tormentor for years. If she continues to hold this attitude of defeat and doesn't do anything to overcome her feelings of inadequacy, she will never be a successful artist who appreciates her own talent and shares it with others.

However, worse than the lost opportunities for fame and the blessing to others are the awful things that have been attracted to her because of what her dominant thoughts have been. Her negative self-talk, or "stinkin thinkin" as Zig Ziglar calls it, has brought into her life all kinds of ills, both physical and mental. It would be far better for her to understand and appreciate the *Law of Attraction* and find a way to acquire a positive attitude; to believe that her talent is good enough to share with others.

Some of the other universal laws, especially those of the spiritual world, are not as easy to understand. But that's OK, because understanding how they work is not as important as learning how to use them to your benefit. Universal laws work the same way every time, so you can easily learn how to use them.

**The *Law of Tithing*** is a universal law of the spiritual world. It is difficult to understand, yet it applies to all of us whether we choose to abide by it or not. It says that if you give of yourself or your possessions out of service, with no expectation of getting anything back in return, then you will receive in return more than you gave. This type of law must be practiced by faith and it takes practice in tithing to observe its benefit.

> *Universal laws ... gravity for example, works the same way every time, in every situation, for every one of us, whether we know about it or are ignorant of it, whether we think about it or not. We accept that because we can prove it. Drop ten pencils, all ten fall to the ground.*
>
> Dan Kennedy

For instance, if you give a portion of your income to a church or charity, it must be done out of service and faith, not expecting anything to come back to you from those you gave it to. You are not buying anything nor exchanging it for any service. The return will be given in some completely unrelated way. Tithing can be seen as an example of not being afraid to fail – to seemingly lose money knowing that your reward will come in full measure from a different source.

Almost all of the successful people that I know of, or have read about, practice tithing to some extent. Some have said that wealth eluded them until they started practicing giving to those in need on a regular basis. This law is one of the only ones in which God challenges people to follow it by saying "test Me in this." The Bible indicates that if you tithe, the flood gates of heaven will be opened and you will have so much that, when poured into your biggest container and it is pressed down and shaken together, it will still be overflowing. Dan Kennedy suggests that "it works because it energizes the subconscious mind with a wealth and success consciousness unlike anything you've ever experienced." But it doesn't matter how it works, just know that it works and it will put you on the fast track to wealth if you abide by it.

If you feel that following universal laws is not important because you don't understand how they work, just remember the seat belt signs posted all along the roads of our country that say "Buckle up – It's the Law." Recently the need for seat belts has been made very real to us, by a major car accident involving close friends. Even now as I write this, our church secretary is in her fourth week of a coma caused by an accident in which she was not wearing her seat belt. Her husband and young son, who were wearing their seatbelts, came out of the accident with only a couple of cuts and bruises. Now they are somberly waiting, hoping, and praying. Circumstances may have been different had she obeyed the law and worn her seat belt.

> *Get a habit, a passion for reading; not flying from book to book, with the squeamish caprice of a literary epicure; but read systematically, closely, thoughtfully, analyzing every subject as you go along, and laying it up carefully and safely in your memory. It is only by this mode that your information will be at the same time extensive, accurate, and useful.*
>
> W. Wirt

You can learn more about universal laws from my next book, *Fast Track to Wisdom* (for previews visit my website www.RandyGilbert.com). In it, I cover a great number of universal laws that I have been learning so that you can better follow them in all areas of your life, not just managing failure. While we are on the subject of reading, I encourage you to become a life long learner. We live during a time when everyone must learn at a very rapid rate or our knowledge base will become obsolete. We must use our time wisely to continuously improve our knowledge and then learn how to build experiences that will rapidly turn that knowledge into wisdom. *Fast Track to Wisdom* will teach you how.

Some people waste hundreds of hours per year listening to noise while they are driving, watching valueless TV programs or absorbing useless information. If you are in that habit, you need to break out of it. Most of those hours would be better spent learning more about your trade or how to improve yourself. Brian Tracy, who has studied and taught about personal achievement for nearly thirty years, says that if we want to just stay even with the new knowledge that is being generated in our field, then we must read at least one hour per day. He advises, "if you want to get ahead in life, you must read at least two hours per day."

Taking Brian Tracy's advice has been one of the best things I have ever done – I recommend you do the same. Read consistently every day if at all possible. It will help you to grow intellectually and it will help you to avoid pitfalls. I feel like I get the equivalent of another Masters degree every year. I find that by setting aside time each day for reading, I can literally learn all that I need to know to do just about anything that I set my mind to.

I listen to audiotapes of the latest business books whenever I am in my car. I subscribe to a couple of book summary companies that record between 25 and 50 of the greatest thinkers of our time. By doing this I can learn the essence of their wisdom and perhaps what has taken them hundreds of hours to learn. I learn a lot more, the ride is less stressful, and it costs me far less than it would have if I were to buy all of the books. Even if I include the expense of the gas for my car, I figure that I would still come out ahead – what a deal!

I also make it a regular habit of listening to *Peter Lowe's Success Talk* audiotapes. Each month Peter interviews a person who has been very successful in their field. What impresses me is that almost every person is very frank about their failures and even points to them as their turning point or their stepping stone to success and fulfillment. I love to hear how they have learned to overcome difficulties and setbacks.

> *Learning is wealth to the poor, an honor to the rich, an aid to the young, and support and comfort to the aged. He who always seeks more light the more he finds, and finds more the more he seeks, is one of the few happy mortals who take and give in every point of time. The tide and ebb of giving and receiving is the sum of human happiness, which he alone enjoys who always wishes to acquire new knowledge, and always finds it.*
>
> Lavater

Many types of therapy situations call for people to help each other. This is a proactive idea for all of us to use. Establish openness among your friends, especially those who are likeminded and positive. This allows for discussions of things that have gone wrong. Do not focus on the down side or set up discussions to have any kind of pity party or gripe session, but rather encourage each other and find the learning experiences and opportunities that come from the problems shared.

Napoleon Hill believed very strongly that *Mastermind Groups* were the key to success for most of the rich and influential people he had interviewed. If you are unfamiliar with how to set them up I recommend that you read the book, *Napoleon Hill's Keys to Success – 17 Principles of Personal Achievement.* I also recommend reading Ben Franklin's autobiography and learning how he effectively set up *Junta Groups* in Philadelphia, where he was able to discuss new ideas among that city's leading business people and statesmen.

The German inventor, Johann Gutenberg, is credited with inventing movable type and therefore, the modern printing press. Gutenberg made it so easy to pass on knowledge that several turn-of-the-century surveys named him as the second millennium's most influential person. He made it so easy to record and pass on information that it is said he is the person who triggered the industrial revolution and moved most of the modern world away from being an agrarian society. Gutenberg made modern schools and universities possible. He was a businessman who knew the value of sharing knowledge and then capitalized on it.

Sir Isaac Newton is cited as being one of the world's smartest people. He was simultaneously the greatest mathematician, scientist, and philosopher during his time. When asked what he attributed his wealth of knowledge to he exclaimed, "it is not because I am particularly smarter than others, but I have learned to stand on the shoulders of giants." You and I must do the same. Even if you feel like a dwarf, you will be able to see further than the giant if you stand on his shoulders. By applying the lessons learned from the giants of the past, you can quickly jump ahead on the learning curve. Additionally, you will avoid making some of the mistakes that might have otherwise set you back years from achieving your own success.

> *A mental giant is one who has his feet firmly planted on the ground, but has ideas that reach to the clouds.*
> Tim Gilbert

Wisdom will lead you to success in every area of your life. In our information age wisdom has become an indispensable attribute for business and civic leaders. Wisdom is essential for young and old. Learn the universal laws of nature and you will put yourself on the fast track to wisdom. This will bring you success, which will in turn bring you joy and abundance.

✓ *Make up your mind to learn from other people's mistakes and failures as well as your own.*

✓ *Try to understand the universal laws and observe how they play into other peoples' lives. It will help you to put your own situation into perspective and it may open your eyes to see how to apply their lessons to your own life.*

✓ *Become a life-long learner. If you don't you will become obsolete and be left behind wondering what went wrong.*

# Strategy 9.

## Turn criticism of failure into a building block of success.

Criticism is both dangerous and powerful. It can confuse your purpose, stop you short of achieving your goals, or even knock the joy out of accomplishing great things in your life. Yet criticism is unavoidable. Therefore, if you never learn to deal appropriately with criticism, then you are left vulnerable to the faults of others as well as your own.

Abraham Lincoln was known to be one of the most criticized Presidents. He was scorned from both sides during the Civil War. He was made to be a fool in the press. Even members of his own Cabinet and his trusted generals ruthlessly maligned him publicly. How did he overcome such attacks? He learned the hard way that you become a small person when you tear people down with criticism, and that is saying a lot considering his physical size. Lincoln learned to never criticize, rather to gain confidence in his own worth when he became the recipient of criticism.

> *I will speak ill of no man, and speak all the good I know of everybody.*
> Benjamin Franklin

Your goal must be to learn to deal with criticism in a constructive manner so that you will be truly unstoppable. If you convert destructive criticism into building blocks for your success, no one will be able to pull you down. When you also learn how to give constructive criticism then you have a tool to create trust and respect.

In his book, *How To Win Friends and Influence People,* Dale Carnegie provides invaluable advice on how to win people over to your point of view. The very first principle he taught was "Don't criticize, condemn, or complain." He talks about the virtues of helping someone to change, improve, or to regulate their behavior;

but he wisely says, "Why not begin on yourself? From a purely selfish standpoint, that is a lot more profitable than trying to improve others – yes, and a lot less dangerous."

Confucius said, "Don't complain about the snow on your neighbor's roof, when your own doorstep is unclean." Jesus warned that we should not try to take the speck out of our brother's eye until we have removed the board from our own. Charles Schwab, a man made very rich from the manufacture of steel and even richer by creating our modern investment system said, "There is nothing else that so kills the ambitions of a person as criticisms from superiors. I never criticize anyone. I believe in giving a person incentive to work. So I am anxious to praise but loath to find fault."

One of the continual battles in the military is between regulars and reservists over regulation haircuts. Dale Carnegie tells of how one Master Sergeant addressed the problem and received both obedience and respect; not by criticizing the reserves and using the traditional threatening mode, but rather by getting them to realize their leadership responsibilities as examples to others. He said, "You know what the regulations say. I am going to get my hair cut today, although it is still much shorter than some of yours. You look at yourself in the mirror, and if you feel you need a haircut to be a good example, we'll arrange time for you to visit the post barbershop."

The Bible teaches us that if we love our children we will teach and discipline them. With discipline comes a pinch of criticism, so St. Paul warns in two separate letters, "Fathers do not exasperate your children." I believe his warning should apply to all superior subordinate relationships, no matter what the age. When you discipline, make sure it is fair and the purpose is understood. When on the receiving end of discipline, don't fight it; accept it for the love and caring that it is.

Our youngest child, now a junior in college, is currently working toward her black belt in karate. She says that she has the most fun and learns the most when an instructor is "picking on her." I'll give you her reasons as she shared them with me.

> Every man I meet is my superior in some way. In that I learn of him.
> Ralph Waldo Emerson

"It's really very simple. When my Senseis (teachers) notice my mistakes, it means that they are paying attention to me. I love personal attention. I think most people feel the same way. In fact, the more nit-picky the Senseis are, the better the compliment. That means they are paying closer attention to me."

"When my Senseis take the time to correct me, I know that they are investing time into my success. Because I was a homeschooler, I know what an effort it is to teach myself. I am all the more eager to get the help I can by learning from others. A Sensei's biting reproof of a block out of place or a kick too low is a very big compliment, no matter how it is disguised. Some compliments come wrapped in harsh words. I don't listen to the way a Sensei is saying it as much as to what the Sensei is really communicating. I 'listen' to what the Sensei is doing and 'watch' what the Sensei means."

"When my Senseis are giving me time and attention I consider it a very valuable thing. I try to give something back in return. When they ask if I am cursing them back under my breath, I honestly say, 'No Sir!' I respect my Senseis for demanding more of me than I would of myself. People can tell the difference between brown-nosing and respect. I believe you should be sincere, give them respect, and don't worry about how it might come across."

Those are words of wisdom from a soon-to-be Black Belt. It is okay to become someone's pet project and thereby receive a little criticism. Consider that person a mentor, even if the relationship is not formalized. Just appreciate your mentor's instruction for the value that it has and pay attention. When your mentor tells you how to do something correctly or better, DO IT. Put in your best effort. My advice to you is that you do not succumb to the frustration of your current inabilities and the criticism that they might draw, so <u>you will not be limited by them for long</u>.

It is definitely in your best interest to follow the advice of someone wiser and more experienced than you. As long as your mentor is experienced, and you put forth your best effort, you will eventually get it right. Your mentor will be rewarded by watching you succeed. Remember, when someone invests their time in improving you, your performance will reflect well on their instruction. Make them proud.

> *Criticism, as a means for benefiting mankind, is meant to be a standard for judging one's own self.*
> Anonymous

As a rule, help other people to recognize their faults only when asked or when its recognized that it is welcome. Most people don't like to be criticized, especially if they are not in a teachable state of mind. I have learned that a person will get into the state of being a good student if, I get in the state of being a good teacher. The Bible advises teachers to, "… clothe yourself with compassion, kindness, humility, meekness, and patience."

The best teachers are those who are humble and want to teach from their own experience. They teach because they have compassion for others and do not want them to have to learn everything the hard way. They also have patience and are willing to endure the learning process. They teach the lesson with meekness, recognizing that the table will be turned someday and they will become the students again, and with kindness, knowing they are not superior, but equal to the student.

The following simple rules will help you to criticize constructively so that even while you are pointing out the faults of others you will be building them up.

1.  Sprinkle in compliments often. It is better to lead from the front with praise and reward. Corrective guidance

measures such as prodding or paddling should be used when absolutely necessary.

2. It is always the behavior you don't like, never the person. Make sure love and trust are intact after the correction is given.

3. Make sure you are open to correction yourself and admit your own mistakes. It not only shows that you are human, but the people you are trying to teach can learn from your mistakes as well as your successes.

4. If the reason for the correction is at your expense (i.e., you were wronged somehow), then make sure apologies and forgiveness happen. This builds trust and commitment to each other.

Even if people who are criticizing or correcting you don't follow the rules for constructive criticism, don't lose the opportunity for your own improvement by being angry with them. Control your emotions and adopt only the ideas they have given you that are pertinent and useful.

> *A great man shows his greatness by the way he treats little men.*
> Thomas Carlyle

A good teacher does not pass judgment on the students, but passes on to the students how to judge their own actions. I remember best the lessons that came to me when I was made to evaluate my own actions. My thoughts go back to one particular incident that deeply embarrassed my father, who had every right to be very angry with me at the time.

The incident happened when I was walking through the schoolyard one beautiful summer day on the Island of Lanai, in Hawaii. I was on my way back from feeding some chickens as a part of a Boy Scout troop project. For some reason I became very curious as to whether the fire alarm worked during the summer months when school was out. Well, IT DID!

I didn't even have a chance to run. I was caught by a teacher working in a nearby classroom and marched to the principal's office. Of course he knew me well and thought I was being my typical troublemaker self. Since he couldn't administer the regular school year punishment, I was turned over to my father. Compared to the principal's usual punishment of pulling weeds, I feared that this was going to be a fate worse than death.

However, this time I was treated differently. I think I must have struck a chord with my father's own mischievous past. Instead of the quick and decisive punishment that I was expecting, my father was calm and deliberate in both his words and his actions. He walked me through an evaluation process that changed my life.

My father believed me when I told him that I had set off the alarm because I was curious. He helped me to see that there were other ways to satisfy my curiosity, if I would just take a few moments to think about them. After discussing several alternatives and realizing how foolish it was to pick the one I did, he helped me to evaluate my own punishment. He wanted me to see that there were different ways of learning a lesson so that the punishment would be equal to the trouble that I had caused and so that I would never forget the lesson. I was not easy on myself.

> *The most noble criticism is that in which the critic is not the antagonist so much as the rival of the author.*
> Benjamin Disraeli

Now when I look back, I remember with fondness the real lesson that I learned that day, which was how to take control of my learning experiences. My father's patience that day helped me to manage my curious nature and put me in charge of my own learning from then on. That was the summer before Seventh Grade. From then on, I feel that I have been accountable to myself for whatever I've needed to learn.

When you take criticism wrong, your confidence in yourself shatters, even as you try to defend your actions. You may become very resentful of the critic and ignore any truth he or she has pointed out. Or perhaps you will give up and resent yourself for being foolish and thinking you might be better than you are.

Becoming an effective teacher and an effective learner are important. The role of teacher may not be distinct when you are trying to help a peer or a peer is trying to help you. However, the rules of criticism still apply. As a learner, concentrate on working for and keeping the positive intent of someone's criticism, while letting the negative fall by the wayside, and your world will become a much more positive and happy place to live. Wisdom is born of criticism if it is used to distinguish between right and wrong. Wisdom is for everyone's success no matter what your age, and you will gain it faster if you make all criticism – constructive criticism.

✓ *Remember, whether you give or receive criticism, make it constructive so that you are building toward success.*

✓ *Even if someone who is criticizing or correcting you doesn't follow the rules for constructive criticism, don't lose the opportunity for your own improvement by being angry with that person. Control your emotions and adopt the ideas that are pertinent and useful.*

✓ *When you find yourself in a position to evaluate others, be an effective teacher by helping your students learn how to judge their own actions so they can manage their own learning experiences.*

# Strategy 10.

# Be a good example – fail in front of your children.

Read almost any newspaper in this country and it will tell you that public schools are doing a poor job with our children. Schools are failing both academically and socially. Up to 50% of children in some inner-city school districts are dropping out, somewhere between their freshman and junior years of high school. And, even for those who do graduate, many of the children still have not learned how to read above the Third or Fourth Grade level.

> *Flexibility is the one trait that softens poverty and adorns riches, for it helps you to be grateful for your blessings and unabashed by misfortune. It also can help you to make beneficial use of every experience of life, whether pleasant or unpleasant.*
>
> Napoleon Hill

In some respects, private schools are not doing much better than public schools. We tried a private school for a while, but even there the curiosity and love for learning that we instilled in our children at an early age was being drummed out by their assembly-line rule-following approach. It is one of the reasons why my wife and I decided to home-school our children.

I recall the incident that became the straw that broke the camel's back. I was called into the principal's office because my son had upset his teacher. It turned out that he had finished a 20-word spelling test in the time that it took his teacher to repeat the second word. When done, he returned to covertly reading a book – one that he was so interested in that he "could not put it down." When his teacher questioned why he was not taking the test with the rest of the class he politely replied that he had already written out all of the words. While being chastised for going ahead, he interrupted his teacher by stating, "What difference does it make? You always say them in the same order and it shouldn't matter what order you say them in because I have memorized them all." When I asked the principal my son's question, he could not give me a satisfactory answer either. They had lost sight of what education was all about.

The children who are ultimately failing in classrooms are not the ones who give the wrong answer, but those who sit there silently without participating; those who are listless and have no questions. They lack desire for learning and don't try. They are satisfied to receive a 'C' grade. They find no purpose in school because there is no relevance to them personally. Such children are the ones who are prone to being chained to mediocrity all of their lives. But is it their fault? What can be done?

My wife is definitely the best teacher I have ever met. She has a knack for making every subject apply to a child's interest area. She says pegging all learning to a person's interest is the key to a good education. Now that we have completed educating our own children, she has become an educational consultant. Incredibly, she has been able to help some children go from receiving straight F's to straight A's in a matter of weeks.

> *What one knows is, in youth, of little moment; they know enough who know how to learn.*
> Henry Adams

I believe that there is something almost magical about aligning learning with students' interest areas. The reason I say that is because when alignment happens students motivate themselves to learn, and if they fail at something they are genuinely interested in, they find out why they failed and then correct their errors. Using a person's interest area also emotionalizes the experience, which acts as an accelerator.

In his book, *Virtual Learning*, Roger Schank, an expert on computer simulation training, says, "If you have a goal, you can learn a lot. You're willing to be corrected for your mistakes and accept 'try this, do that' advice in order to achieve your goal. Remember, though, that goals only work this way if they are your own rather than someone else's."

Some people succeed against all odds. I grew up in Hawaii and one of my classmates, Christian Riese Lassen, is now a very rich and famous painter of Hawaiian seascapes. However, getting good grades in school was a terrible problem for him. Whenever the "surf was up" he was absent or it kept him from doing his homework. The only classes it seemed he did really well in were art classes.

My eldest sister was in one of Chris's art classes and I remember her saying that he did a replica painting of Leonardo da Vinci's *Mona Lisa*. Their teacher was astonished and could not believe how good it was. My sister now says that she knew then that he was going to be a famous painter. Why couldn't the rest of us see it? His classmates and teachers would have voted him "least likely to succeed in life" because of his lack of interest in school and his failing grades. However, his passion and love for art and the sea were putting him on the fast track to riches and fame. He was fortunate; in spite of a school system that largely ignored his passion; he took charge of educating himself in what he loved and in what would eventually bring him true success.

If you feel that you are failing as a parent because you have an energetic "problem" child who won't study – DON'T! It is often the children labeled troublemakers, those who seem to defy rules and strike out with their own ideas of how to do things so that they are fun and interesting who will some day make you so proud that you'll feel your chest about to burst. Most overly energetic children are very intelligent and have not been shown how to direct their energy in useful ways that will captivate their attention.

St. Paul wrote in two letters the following parental warning; "Do not exasperate your children, that they may become angry and lose heart, but bring them up in the instruction of the Lord." We as parents need to channel their seemingly boundless energy; not make rules against it. Find out what your child likes to do. Discover what his or her passion is and then find a way to direct every learning experience toward your child's passion. If God has instilled a passion in your child and you fight against it, you may find yourself fighting God Himself and you will never have peace of mind if you do that.

Another reason that Cathy is such a good teacher is that she teaches children that it is OK to make mistakes. She sometimes pretends to make mistakes just to show them that everyone makes mistakes and you can learn from them. What is important, she tells them, is that you try your best because eventually you will do your best.

I believe that parents and teachers need to be free to fail in front of children in order to teach them how to fail correctly. Children need to see that it is OK to make mistakes in order to learn, even for grown-ups. They need to know that they won't be punished for asking questions, especially when they don't understand a lesson. They also need to know they won't be punished or laughed at when they give an incorrect answer to a question. It is all a part of the learning experience.

Drs. Cloud and Townsend, give this advice in *Boundaries With Kids*: "Disabuse your child of the notion she can get around failure. Make failure her friend. Talk about the dumb things you did at work or at home. Don't be defensive when a family member points out another mindless thing you did. Be careful not to give your child the impression that you love her perfect, performing parts more than you do her mediocre, stumbling parts."

> *A good character is, in all cases, the fruit of personal exertion. It is not created by external advantages; it is no necessary appendage of birth, wealth, talents, or station; but it is the result of one's own endeavors – the fruit and reward of good principles manifested in a course of virtuous and honorable action.*
> J. Hawes

We taught our children not to be afraid of failing; in fact, they were given the responsibility of grading their own test papers. We set the guidelines for them and they measured their own performance according to expectations. If they scored anything less than a 90, they had to review the section again and learn what they had missed the first time through. We never worried about them cheating, because who would they be cheating? They learned through practice, in a non-threatening way, what 'A' performance was. Their mistakes taught them quickly and they continued to be interested because they were responsible for their own learning experience.

My wife now works with the children of migrant workers. We have noted that if they are less than eight years of age, many of them pick up conversational English in about one year. Little children seem to learn quickly because they are not afraid to repeat the words they've learned over and over again, even if they are not pronouncing them correctly and their grammar is poor. Fortunately for them, young children are not afraid to make mistakes.

I took Spanish for two years in high school. Why is it that I did not learn to speak it? I now think it is because I was afraid to speak Spanish. I believe that those of us who are thirteen years and older are afraid to make mistakes in front of others, so we shy away from practicing the new language verbally. I am now attending a conversational Spanish class that my wife teaches in the evenings. She helps everyone to feel comfortable, as if we are one big happy family. I am now learning to speak the language more quickly (*más rapidamente*) because I am less afraid of saying something silly in front of people I don't know.

> *I started out as a secretary at a television station in Houston. Don't be afraid to start small ... You can learn a lot faster at local TV stations and smaller companies, where you are allowed to make mistakes.*
>
> M.L. Flynn,

If you love your children you should be willing to fail with them in order that they might learn. Help them to discover their passion or interest area. It may take a while and it might be by "trial and error." Let them help make a decision and then, for better or worse, live with the consequences, at least until the lesson is learned, and then move on.

For example, if your daughter shows a particularly strong interest in pets, she might want to become a veterinarian some day. You would be helping her out immensely if you allowed her to explore her interest. You might do this by helping her to purchase some pets and teach her how to be responsible for them. If you found yourself doing all of the caring for the animals then you both would know that it was a passing fancy. Help your children learn that trial and error is OK.

Trust me; whatever it is that your children settle on as an interest or passion will be worth every penny or ounce of energy spent discovering it. Your children will then have something that will bring them joy and will teach them wisdom more quickly. I did not really discover my passion until my children were older and they watched me "fail in front of them." We are all better for it. I know what my passion is; and, they are unafraid of the trial and error that it will take to discover their dreams too. Wisdom truly is for young and old.

- ✓ *Children (and grown-ups) learn much better and faster if everything they learn is tied to their area of interest. Do not depend on school systems to help your children discover the joy of learning; parents should do whatever it takes to help.*

- ✓ *Teach your children that it is OK to make mistakes; in fact, the more mistakes they make doing the things they love, the faster they will learn wisdom.*

# *Strategy 11.*

# *Not getting caught doesn't mean you didn't fail.*

It seems that people are born with a natural tendency to be afraid of admitting they have problems. We all have a tendency to want to hide problems in two ways. The first is hiding problems from ourselves by outright refusing to acknowledge them. Shakespeare wrote, "to thine own self be true, and it must follow, as the night the day, thou canst then be false to any man." When we are afraid of our failures we have a tendency to lie about them. However, not admitting that a problem exists doesn't make it go away. Rather, lying usually makes matters worse.

> *An honest reputation is within the reach of all; they obtain it by social virtues and doing their duty – This kind of reputation, though neither brilliant nor startling, is often the most conducive to happiness.*
> Duclos

When we cover up problems, we are stealing from ourselves. We are stealing our reputations and our time, because it will take a lot longer to learn the requisite lesson. But the opposite is true; when we admit the truth about the problem or fault, we are building our reputations and we are also open to learning at a more rapid rate.

I recommend that you decide right now that lying to yourself is harmful and that you won't do it. If you have fallen into the habit of lying, then look at it as a character trait that needs to be replaced and follow the character-improving advice in Strategy 15.

The second way people hide problems is, of course, from others. "It is OK to do whatever you want so long as you don't get caught" is a prevalent but dangerous mentality. It is a trap that you should be careful not to fall into. When we hide problems from others, they don't go away. It is like sweeping the dust under the rug.

Eventually problems must be dealt with and we are wasting valuable time, energy, and sometimes money with schemes meant to cover up problems rather than deal with them.

Guard your reputation by having a good sense of right and wrong within. Your code of conduct must be rooted and grounded by integrity into the very core of your being. When this is the case, despite all else that happens to you through any kind of failing, you will be able to maintain your reputation. You will need your good reputation to maintain trust and good relationships if a major disaster strikes you or your business.

Do not compromise your values. When you are trying to figure out how to turn a failure around, your values are not negotiable. Don't let any one counsel you to lie, cheat, or steal in order to improve a situation. It won't work! In fact, it is almost guaranteed to make things worse. The *Law of Compensation* will not yield for you; you will be required at some point in time to make restitution. As the saying goes, "either pay now or pay later." It is far better to admit a problem exists and not yield on any of your essential values.

Not long ago I had a conversation with a person who was in charge of safety for a large group of chemical plants. He had spoken at a public meeting in a West Virginia town. The meeting had been arranged to help the people of that particular town realize the benefits of locating a chemical plant in their area. He said he began to speak on how safe the plant would be and gave them lots of statistics on how few accidents there had been in other plants similar to the one that would be built there.

In the midst of the talk, a woman stood up and interrupted him saying, "Sir, we know that the chemicals that will be brought in are dangerous and could kill us all. What we want to know is, what are you going to do to make this plant safe? How are you going to handle the problems when they come up, because they will come up, you've just shown us that they can."

That woman was very astute. She realized that problems would always arise; they could not be hidden behind safety statistics. She felt that she would trust the chemical company a whole lot more if they would not hide the potential problems. She wanted the problems brought out into the open to see how they would be dealt with. My friend changed his talk right there on the spot.

He spoke of what plans the company had in place for dealing with potential problems. This particular company had a safety program that always evaluated what the optimum safety condition should be, not just what the minimum requirements were. They realized that minimum requirements were not sufficient.

This particular chemical company built up the trust of the community that evening by explaining their program, not their safety statistics. They won the approval of the town to build the plant. This kind of openness and honesty builds trust, which is critical for all businesses to have.

> *It has been the glory of the great masters in all arts to confront and to overcome; and when they had overcome the first difficulty, to turn it into an instrument for new conquests over new difficulties; thus to enable them to extend the empire of science.*
>
> J. Hawes

A problem does not have to be a major catastrophe. Sometimes it is beneficial to look at what some of the causes are that contribute to a failure and try to prevent those causes from happening. The U.S. aviation industry is one of the safest and is the pacesetter for safety worldwide because the U.S. Federal Aviation Administration (FAA) defines a failure as a "near-miss," or something that could have contributed to (caused) an accident even though one did not occur.

The FAA has a near-miss reporting system that is designed to let people "tell on themselves" without repercussion. This is a great system that encourages honesty and openness for the benefit of all (especially for us passengers), and it removes all liability from the person making the report, even if the FAA through regular channels becomes aware of the situation.

I believe the FAA's near-miss reporting system can be used as a model for our personal and business lives. In fact, I believe that near misses are preferred types of problems because they can provide just as much, if not more, help to us in eliminating costly failures from our lives. Let me explain the FAA system and its benefits.

The person who wants to make a report initiates it by filling out a simple form that is readily available. It is sent to a third party organization that is contracted to collect the information and keep the database. The problem is then logged, categorized, stripped of its sensitive information and then entered into a huge database. The database is then used to more quickly spot bad trends that are happening in the industry and to pinpoint where improvements need to be made before they become major catastrophes.

You might be thinking to yourself, what an excellent win-win situation for the aviation industry and the FAA, but there is more. When I was active in the Coast Guard, I was promoting a similar system for the marine industry. During my research into the FAA's system, I learned that there was an additional unplanned benefit. Just before the informant's name and contact information are discarded, a call is made to the person to make sure that all of the pertinent information has been collected and that it is correct.

> *Bad thoughts are worse enemies than lions and tigers; for we can keep out of the way of wild beasts, but bad thoughts win their way everywhere. The cup that is full will hold no more; keep your hearts full of good thoughts, so that bad thoughts may find no room to enter.*
>
> Bp. Porteus

Here is the key: the person making the call is a retired pilot or air traffic controller. The verification telephone call provides a wonderful opportunity for empathizing, "I had that happen to me one time" and counseling, "Let me tell you what I did to solve the problem."

WOW! That is a win-win-win situation. The person who has made the report learns, in a non-threatening way, what he or she might personally be able to do correctly should a similar situation arise. Those of us who fly a lot should be jumping with joy for such a system.

We can take up the same practice as the aviation industry no matter what our situation or occupation. It doesn't have to be a huge program or database. Just follow the simple steps. Admit when you have experienced a problem. Report it without repercussion or fault. Analyze and classify what caused it. Find out what you can do personally to prevent the problem. Provide the information to those who might be able to improve the process or entire system.

In recent years, the marine industry has been discovering a need to exceed the minimum regulations. Unfortunately, it has been at the expense of thousands of lives lost on oceangoing passenger ferries. The ships were legal, but not safe enough to keep them from capsizing and sinking when they flooded their car decks. Many of us predicted these tragedies because of "near-misses" that had happened. Unfortunately for many, nothing was done at that time. Ignoring the problem didn't make it go away. Now that the accidents have happened, rules have changed. Fortunately for us, those particular designs are no longer a legal design method for new ferries.

> *Unlike wine, problems do not get better with age.*
> Old wise saying

Admitting problems and mistakes when they are detected is a lesson for all of us to learn. Make open and honest evaluations of what can go wrong. Then develop plans to prevent potential problems as best you can. But remember, there can be no doubt that both wisdom and success come out of struggles, adversity, and failures. I do not hold to the belief that people make fewer mistakes as they get older; rather, I believe that we make different mistakes as we continue gaining wisdom in different areas of our lives.

✓ *Be true to yourself and admit when you have problems or have made a mistake.*

✓ *Don't be afraid to tell others that a problem exist, especially if they can help solve the problem.*

✓ *If you want to have a very low level of risk, then you need to report near-misses and events that might contribute to problems, then prevent them from happening.*

# *Part III*

# *Shatter the Glass Ceiling*

*Wow! This plant must have overheard me telling my children that nothing is impossible to those who believe.*

**Foreword to Part III**

It was still thought to be impossible when John F. Kennedy bravely announced at the beginning of his Presidency, that by the end of the decade, Americans would be walking on the moon. President Kennedy believed in it and inspired others to believe in it. Plans were made, resources dedicated, and orders given – and so it was achieved in June of 1969, six months before the end of the decade.

That is just one among thousands of examples of how the seemingly impossible can be made possible by those who believe. I love to hear the stories of those who broke through the barriers that people had at one time thought to be invincible. The book-shelves are filled with such stories.

Nothing is impossible to you if you are willing to think correctly and put forth the right level of effort. Success and abundance is not impossible for you, but no one said it was going to be easy. If others have been able to overcome handicaps and disadvantages then you can too.

I once thought working for myself to be impossible. Success was on the other side of a thick glass ceiling. In the mind of the pessimist, if it hadn't been done before, it couldn't be done. The fear of failure strikes out and paralyzes the pessimist.

I was constrained by my own thinking. I had to gather my courage and shatter the glass. I had to rid myself of the fear of failure. I found the courage to do that by finding my major purpose in life. I became convinced that if I used my talents and abilities in this single pursuit, I would succeed.

The strategies of Part III focus on helping you to break through whatever barriers might be holding you back from achieving your dreams and goals. You will also learn how to optimize your life so you can be all you can be and thereby live a happier and more abundant life.

# Strategy 12.

# *Rid yourself of the fear of failure.*

The fear of failure can be paralyzing and even dangerous. Have you ever been afraid of getting shots? Your mind holds on to the image of the needle drawing closer and closer to your exposed arm. You tense up. Your eyes are wide, you wonder at the unseemly large size of the needle. The metal is cold and then hot as it is pressed into your skin. As the needle penetrates your skin the pain is excruciating and numbing sending a shock to your brain.

You can't avoid the shot, but you can avoid some of the pain. Let's analyze what causes the pain and how you can minimize it. I'm afraid that the needle is an integral part of the injection process so it can't be avoided. So, now look at the situation to see what can be changed. Don't tense up! It's that simple. It's a proven fact that when you're relaxed, shots don't hurt as much. Take control of your mind and don't dread the visit to the doctor's office days in advance. Relax your arm, look away from the needle; be curious about how the needle feels instead of flinching, and then you won't be sore and bruised the next day.

My wife and I hosted a Japanese foreign exchange student for a year and had a wonderful experience. My wife has a lot of experience teaching English as a Second Language (ESL) and it really helped our "adopted daughter" to learn English quickly. Recently, the director of the program called us because one of the newly arrived students would not speak any English. The director was afraid that if this student wasn't able to speak enough English to attend the high school that she might have to be sent back to Japan. The director was hoping that my wife could help with an ESL assessment to see if the student had sufficient aptitude.

Cathy wasn't home at the time so I asked a few questions about what the student was like and if she had any difficulty speaking in her own language.  The director said that when she spoke in Japanese that she was very animated and sure of herself.  The student also had very good grades in all her subjects while in Japan, especially her English classes.

> *Do the thing you fear and you shall have power over it.*
> Ralph Waldo Emerson

The director said that the student had referred to herself as a perfectionist.  She had told the director through an interpreter that she would only play a piece of music on the piano for others when she could play it perfectly.  I told the director, "that is where her problem is; the fear of failure."  She is so afraid of making a mistake with her English that she is making an even BIGGER mistake of not talking at all.  I suggested the strategy that I have outlined in this book.  It worked like a charm and in no time at all, and to everyone's delight, she was chattering away in broken English and ready to start school here in the U.S.  It was not an ESL problem; it was a <u>fear of failure</u> problem.

Dan Kennedy, one of my favorite authors on business success says in his book, *No B.S. Business Success*, "I've come to the conclusion that the way you deal with failure controls your future opportunities to deal with success.  In fact, it is through failure that you learn to overcome the fear of failure!  And once experience demonstrates that failure isn't fatal, you can move on, full steam ahead."

Dan also gives statistics to prove that behind every entrepreneurial success there are an average of 3.8 embarrassing failures.  In fact, the more successful the person, the worse his or her failures were in both number and severity.  A successful entrepreneur learns to acknowledge failures, then understand and control feelings toward them, and then refocus energies toward extracting the positive opportunities and using them to reach goals.

I discovered the best way to remove the fear of failure is to replace it with something else.  I learned that your conscious mind can only dwell on one thing at a time so, by the *Law of Substitution*, I could replace fear with love. The Bible teaches, "… perfect love casts out all fear." When I began to focus my life on loving and serving my family and the people around me, I lost my fear of failure. You can do the same. Just love the people that you care about so much that you are willing to go to any length for them – even failure.

> *No man is more unhappy than the one who is never in adversity; therefore, the greatest affliction of life is never to be afflicted.*
>
> Anonymous

In the Bible it says, "Greater love has no one than this, that one lay down his life for his friends." I learned in the military that I was serving my country and its citizens (my friends) in this way. In the Coast Guard, as in other services, there are plenty of opportunities to "lose your life for a friend."

Countless men and women have lost their lives in search and rescue missions and in battle. When you are able to put your life on the line, then the fear of failure in the routine activities of life seem small and trivial. This type of passion, to serve your fellow man at any cost, drives fear out and you are literally guaranteed to succeed in whatever you do.

Jesus spent a lot more time talking with those who needed help than he did with people who thought they were successful. He taught them how to overcome their problems. He went to the blind, the lame, the sinners and tax collectors (worst of the lot) so He could help them overcome their failures. Did He just heal the ailments that they thought they had? No, he healed *all* of their problems; physical, mental, and spiritual. It is not that the others didn't need help, but they wouldn't admit to needing any help. Jesus even told them they were blind and lame spiritually, but they refused to listen to Him, they didn't want His help.

Some people thought the death of Jesus was His defeat, but nothing could be further from the truth. It became His greatest success. He was so focused on loving us that He put all thought of failure out of His mind. When He was in the garden on the night He was betrayed He prayed, "if there is a way this cup can be taken from me, but not My will, Your will be done." From that decision point on he was solidly confident about what He had to do – He set fear aside and just DID IT! In our own small ways, you and I must reach that decision point too. If you want to rid yourself of the fear of failure, then choose to fulfill your mission, your purpose, and your passion in life for the sake of loving and serving others.

If we are to have a healthy view of our lives we must allow examination of all areas. How are you doing with your mental thoughts and beliefs? Do they keep you from having what you would like? Do they hold you back from really getting good at your personal mission in life? Review your spiritual life. Do you have the faith that you need, or the hope, or the inner peace? If not, why not?

Please let me encourage you not to be afraid of examining any of those areas of your life. The Bible is the primary yardstick that I use for self-examination. But besides that, I read extensively about what other people have learned, which I have found to be very helpful. It not only exposes me to smart people, but many of their ideas have been "tested by fire" and have put me on the fast track to wisdom.

> *All fear is painful, and when it conduces not to safety, is painful without use. Every consideration, therefore, by which groundless terrors may be removed, adds something to human happiness.*
>
> Johnson

The fear of failure prevents change, which prevents improvement. Admit you have faults, fears, and "dark sides," and then openly and honestly deal with them. It is a much better way to go. Jesus told the story of two sinners – one who admitted his sin and was repentant (wanting to change) and the other who knew of other people's faults but not his own. The repentant man would not even approach the front of the sanctuary, but stood in the back, begging for forgiveness. The second, more pious man walked boldly to the altar and expressed his gratitude for not having any faults. When Jesus asked those listening which of the two they thought would be forgiven and helped, they correctly chose the first man, who was direct and honest about his failings.

The honest and repentant man probably went on to live a very happy and prosperous life, free of whatever fault had caused him such sorrow. The unrepentant man probably remained chained to his life of mediocrity. My experiences in life have brought me across such individuals, they seemed to always be bitter and blameful of others for their own shortcomings; never able to admit to the reality of the situation. You must act in the same manner as the repentant man, admit to the failings and shortcomings that have been exposed and make the needed changes to your life.

Do not look at sorrow as a reason for self-pity; it is not. Our Creator wisely gave us sorrow so we could enjoy the highest plane of existence and use our superiority moderately and wisely. When you allow sorrow to work in your life, you will have the capacity for genius, provided you understand it as a welcome source of discipline. From the depths of sorrow you will discover immense powers of courage that will help you overcome the failures and trials that life brings. Like failure, sorrow will bring the seed of an equivalent joy if you learn to have the right attitude and nurture your seed into a flower of triumph and beauty.

> *You will find it less easy to uproot faults, than to choke them by gaining virtues.*
> Ruskin

There is no type of failure that is a disgrace if you have done your best. Every game ends with winners and losers. Is it a disgrace to lose? No, of course not. If professional athletes don't see losing as a disgrace then why should you or I? They don't see it as a disgrace because they know that each game, whether they win or lose, is a learning experience. They will get better and have another chance to come out on top in the next game.

There are several other notable ways for you to rid yourself of fear. Ralph Waldo Emerson said, "Do the thing you fear and the death of fear is certain." Brian Tracy picks up on this and coaches people to do what you fear over and over again until it becomes just another task. He says that it is particularly true for public speaking, which studies show that more than half the people in the U.S. fear more than dying. Dale Carnegie is still the most renowned teacher of the art of public speaking. He lives on in his many books, particularly ones like, *How to Develop Self-Confidence & Influence People by Public Speaking,* and he continues to teach us how to overcome our fear of speaking out in any type of forum. His basic four-part advice is:

*First:  Start with a Strong and Persistent Desire.*
*Second:  Know Thoroughly What You Are Going To Talk About.*
*Third:  Act Confidently. And*
*Fourth:  Practice, Practice, Practice.*

Noah St. John in his book, *Permission to Succeed,* teaches that fear is a natural human tendency meant to warn us when we are approaching danger. He likens it to having a concerned mother. He recommends that you act accordingly, by acknowledging the fear, doing what is necessary to guard against any real harm, and then telling your fear not to worry, everything will be OK.

It is up to you to choose which way is best for you to address your fears. The thing that matters is that you do address them. I recommend that you take a proactive view of them and see that they can help you to sharpen your skills. They can give you a greater desire to become really good at what you were meant to do.

Fear can paralyze. It can prevent you from taking advantage of opportunities. When allowed to rule freely it can even prevent you from preparing for opportunities. It is no way to win. There is a certain rabbit that lives at the end of my long gravel driveway. Very often when I am either coming or going, I find the rabbit sitting in the middle of the drive nibbling the grass. As I approach, it dashes first one way and then the other. At times it is off the road to one side and then dashes back across to the other side. It seems to be so afraid of choosing the wrong side that sometimes I must come to a complete stop as it sits quivering and looking frantically both ways, frozen by indecision and fear.

When I lost my fear of failure I found my courage to make decisions – it gave me the freedom to move forward and succeed. I stopped worrying about my ideas and how they came across to people.

Albert Einstein, the man chosen above all others by *Time* magazine as the person to have had the greatest impact during the twentieth century, said, "If at first the idea is not absurd, then there is no hope for it."   I thought to myself, if people called the ideas of this great genius absurd, then why wouldn't I expect people to think my ideas a little crazy?   And if it took a great man like Abraham Lincoln a whole lifetime of failures and setbacks to become a great success (a U.S. President), then who am I to feel that I should not be subject to adversity on my way to achieving my goals and objectives?

> *He that can heroically endure adversity will bear prosperity with equal greatness of soul; for the mind that cannot be defected by the former is not likely to be transported with the latter.*
>
> Fielding

Breaking yourself of the fear of failure is the best way to shatter the glass ceiling that has kept you from soaring up with the eagles. Don't settle for scratching in the dirt like a turkey.  Recognize who you are – you are God's creation, made in His image, destined for success.  The thoughts of fear are a trick from the enemy to steal that success from you.  Believe in yourself.  Be passionate in your service to others and your fears will melt away like ice off a roof on a sunny spring day.

✓ *Identify the fears that are holding you back and deal with them by learning all about them – it will give you power over them.*

✓ *Replace thoughts of fear with thoughts and deeds based on love and a desire to serve others – then there will be no stopping you.*

✓ *Confront your inadequacies and overcome them by dealing with them directly. Replace character problems with essential values and virtues.*

# Strategy 13.

## Have an appetite for failure.

From the very beginning and all the way to the end, life gives you problems and struggles for your own good. I have learned that I must not deny myself the lessons and avoid the exercising of my character that failures bring. This concept may not be easy, particularly if you are in an organization that does not reward high achievers who make mistakes because they are willing to push the envelope and learn from their failures. Some organizations have misapplied the total quality management (TQM) principles as they were intended by Deming and have reduced their tolerance for possible failure, instead of managing it.

> *Adversity has ever been considered the state in which a man most easily becomes acquainted with himself, then, especially, being free from flatterers.*
>
> Johnson

The Coast Guard performance-rating system that was in place before I retired was sometimes an example of rewarding mediocrity. The rating system was failure intolerant, because if someone failed in even one small performance area, it was viewed as a "black mark" against him. Just one black mark put a person in the danger zone of being passed over for promotion and eventually losing his or her job. Even if that person had just made a huge leap in performance due to having learned a valuable lesson, the stigma of having failed was present and irreversible.

Therefore the system seemed to engender mediocrity in some commands. People became averse to taking risks. A type of paranoia of failure set in. This is not good, because logic would tell you that if the Coast Guard got rid of the people who were willing to take chances in order to achieve more for the service, then eventually the Coast Guard would be left only with those who were satisfied with a mediocre status quo in the ranks.

The Coast Guard is not alone in this dilemma. I have talked with many people from other government agencies and business organizations. They too have experienced that mediocrity is rewarded, rather than banished. My hope is that senior officers and executives from such organizations might read this book. If you are one of them, please understand that failures can be managed and high achievers can actually be rewarded if they have learned from their failures.

If you are in such an organization, do your best and find a way to reward yourself. Look at the big picture; if there is no way to change this aspect of the organization, you might be better off either on your own or in a new organization that wants you to grow and succeed.

I have learned to appreciate problems and struggles. I believe that struggles were created to strengthen us; it is the same for all of nature. One of my family's favorite places to visit is Colonial Williamsburg, Virginia. We have been there many times and always come away having learned new and interesting things. On one trip we learned a great lesson in success from the wheelwright (the person who makes wagon wheels). He said that he made sure the wood he used was taken from a tree that was out in a field by itself. He said the strongest trees aren't those protected by the others in the forest. He needed wood that had been strengthened by having to struggle against the wind. The wheelwright was confident that, if he had wood hardened by the forces of nature, he could bend and mold the arc-shaped segments into a wheel that would not fail, even under heavy loads.

> *There is no merit where there is no trial; and till experience stamps the mark of strength, cowards may pass for heroes, and faith for falsehood.*
>
> A. Hill

I believe that if we were to remove the struggles of life, we would at the same time remove in the same proportion our opportunities for success. The education through trial and error, the strengthening of our character through adversity, all add up cumulatively from every experience. Therefore, we should not shun failure, but rather accept it for what it is – a chance to be a better and stronger person.   Learn how to manage failures so that you will become strong in your body, mind, and spirit.

Be proactive and learn what your appetite for failure is.   I recommend that you work to increase your appetite for failure, because even if it is at the cost of making a few mistakes along the way, it will bring you success.

In his book *Permission to Succeed,* Noah St. John likens the people who never give themselves permission to succeed as those having the malady of anorexia.   He also indicates that in order to overcome the anorexia and give yourself permission to succeed, one most overcome the fear of failure.   In other words, you must first give yourself permission to fail.

Some situations involve risks of problems that will not go away. Therefore, some problems cannot be solved, but only managed.  If we do not have an appetite for such problems or give ourselves permission to expose ourselves to the possibility of failure, we would virtually eliminate success from the situation and be forever chained to mediocrity, or worse.

Increase your appetite for success and learn how to manage the failures that are sure to accompany you in your achievement.  A battle could not be won if a field commander was not willing for any of his men to die.  A quarterback would never throw the ball if he were not willing to allow the chance of an interception.

A ship may seem safe tied up to the dock, but what good is it?  It is only a very high expense to the owner.  If we did not allow oil to be shipped into the United States, our businesses and personal lives would be altered immeasurably.  Our whole Country's economic system would be in jeopardy.  Shipping oil cannot be stopped.  As long as we are shipping oil there is always the chance for an oil spill.

The acronym ALARP stands for <u>As Low As Reasonably Possible</u>. The oil transportation industry has learned to use ALARP to manage the risks that shipping oil brings.  The rest of the people in our Country and the world get to enjoy the opportunities oil brings. An organization or a person who does not allow for the possibility of failure is doomed to mediocrity.

> *People do not succeed as often as wanted because they are unwilling to chance failure as often as needed.*
> Randy Gilbert

The best way to shatter the glass ceiling that is holding you back is to learn how to fail often enough so that your failures eventually lead you to abundance and success. Wherever you find a successful person you will find a person who has struggled in life and has learned to manage those failures.  By learning to have an appetite for more failures, rather than avoid them, you can grow beyond your limitations – and you will find there is no limit to the success you can have.

✓ *If you want to be truly successful, you must become a strong individual.  Learn to appreciate nature's way of things and take on a positive attitude toward the failures, defeats, and struggles that will come your way.*

✓ *Some problems in life cannot be solved, but only managed. There are plenty of opportunities that come out of both kinds. You will become a much happier person if you give yourself permission to chance failure, because in so doing you will be giving yourself permission to succeed.*

# Strategy 14.

# Use failures to optimize your life.

There is no chance for any sailing vessel to win a race like the Americas Cup unless it has been thoroughly optimized. Every aspect of design has to be analyzed and tested to make sure its performance is the best it can be. There can be no extra weight through over-design because it will slow the boat down. On the other hand, none of the rigging, braces, or structure can be less than 100 percent capable of supporting the strain that is expected at maximum wind speeds. If one of the wires that support the mast is too weak and it breaks before the maximum speed can be attained, then its size must be increased. If it is increased too much, then the extra weight of the long heavy wire begins to slow the boat down and that is not good either. There must be a keen balance.

During the race the crew maximizes the boat's speed by managing every aspect of the sails so that they draw out every bit of energy from the wind. This requires optimizing everything during the race too. If the boat is leaning way over in a strong wind and a crewmember begins to panic before the boat has reached the limits of what it was designed for, then that crewmember has to be retrained or even replaced by one less afraid. Everything must be optimized.

> *There's no doubt in my mind that if I spent eighteen hours a day with the business and none with my family and none with the community, the business would be worse off. If you don't lead some semblance of a balanced life, you are going to make poor decisions in all parts of your life.*
> Elliot Hoffman

I have learned that if I want to succeed in life, I need to get beyond the "good enough" mentality – I have to break the bonds of mediocrity and begin to optimize my life. The goal is peak performance. However, there are things that I do that are over-designed. Those things "weigh me down" and keep me from performing at my optimum. There are also aspects of my life that have been too skimpy. Such things have caused unreliable areas in my life, which have held me back. The key to knowing what they are is paying attention to every aspect of my life. Like a sailboat, I need to get out into a good strong breeze and gain experience. Then I must make changes and try again.

When I was stationed in Hawaii I taught my family how to sail, courtesy of Hickam Air Force Base recreational yacht harbor. It made for superb family weekend outings that were a lot of fun. It also taught my children a great lifetime skill and was jam-packed with other educational lessons.

We started out by learning how to sail small dinghies. They were easily capsized (tipped over). If you don't know what you are doing, which you don't when you are first starting out, you find yourself in the water with the task of "righting" the boat and bailing it out. We all got wet several times during the first couple of trips around the course.

We started with the dinghies because everything you do makes a difference. The slightest wrong movement to the tiller or sail will threaten to capsize the boat. Failures happened often at first, which tested the limits of our skill and knowledge. But since we knew exactly what we had done to capsize the boat, we learned very quickly how to sail. While sailing the dinghies, we remained in the harbor where it was safe to capsize. I wish all of life's lessons could be as good and as much fun.

My family quickly moved up to larger boats. Each time we mastered a skill we would go for a "checkout ride" with one of the instructors at the boat harbor. Our final graduation present to ourselves was an inter-island trip from Oahu to Lanai, which also took us past Kahoolave, Molokini, Maui, and Molokai. Our track line took us through the Nawiliwili Channel, which is known to be one of the roughest in the world. The trip gave us a chance to push the boat, and ourselves, to the design limits. We found that neither was ready for the Americas Cup, but I am positive that it is an experience none of us will ever forget.

Every person has his or her own design limits; what are yours? How will you know what they are unless you test them? I believe failures happen in our lives so that we can have the opportunity to find out what they are and so that we might be able to optimize them. They help you to get to know yourself. They teach you how to control your thoughts. They teach you how to make adjustments. In short, your failures teach you how to keep improving until you reach your optimum.

> *If at first you do not succeed, try, try again.*
> Old adage

I have found that it is beneficial to set 'stretch goals' that strengthen me, but don't put too much of a strain on me. Setting stretch goals is similar to exercising. You need to do a little each day or two. If you try to exercise too much at once, you might injure yourself. It is best to develop a lifelong habit of maintaining your body and mind in good health. You should consistently and intelligently make improvements.

Live with the idea that you will not always do well at first, but never accept it as your best effort. Acceptance of less than the best is not the goal of learning to manage failures; nothing could be further from the truth.

Dan Kennedy, a prolific business author and marketing guru says, "nothing is worth doing if it is not worth doing badly at first." You would not be able to launch out in a new direction if you did not give yourself the opportunity to do poorly at first. The key is to learn as quickly from your mistakes as possible.

The following is a recommended exercise to help you make improvements in your life. Make a list of things that you are doing that you feel you could improve. Now look at each thing as objectively as possible and plan out how you can approach each one. What do you need to improve? It is not easy to admit the things that you are not good at, but you cannot improve if you will not face the truth. Look at it from a positive frame of mind and be proud that you are willing to make the effort. Make sure the things in your plan are in "bite-size" increments and then take action on them. Check your list every so often. Cross off the things you have conquered and add new ones so your mind is constantly seeking ways to improve. Also, don't forget to reward yourself for each goal you achieve – it really helps.

> *You have absolute control over but one thing, and that is your thoughts. ... This divine prerogative is the sole means by which you may control your own destiny. If you fail to control your own mind, you may be sure you will control nothing else.*
>
> Napoleon Hill

If there is an area in your life that just doesn't seem to be performing well any more, then ask yourself Brian Tracy's zero-based thinking question: "Knowing what I now know, would I do it again if I had to start over?" If the answer to that question is 'No,' then it would be wise to figure out how to STOP DOING IT. What you are doing is probably holding you back from accomplishing your true major purpose in life. It is better that you admit you have a problem sooner rather than later. As the old adage goes, "Problems are not like wine. They don't get better with age."

Sometimes it is our own belief system that holds us back from reaching our optimum potential. If your thoughts go unchanged, you will never achieve your highest goals and success will elude you. Your beliefs must be replaced or modified so they won't hold you back. How do you know that you can't get better if you haven't tried hard enough or tried enough times? And, how do you know that you can't be the best, or at least one of the best in your field or business, if you have not stretched yourself beyond your self-imposed limits?

Expanding your belief system is like shattering the glass ceiling. Women in business and in the military are finally realizing the limitations they experienced in their careers are glass ceilings that can be broken. Some have discovered that advancement is really created in their own minds. Many have shattered the glass and are moving on to optimize their chances for success.

I reread a book that was very helpful to me as a young officer in the Coast Guard. It's called *The Magic of Thinking Big*, written by David Schwartz. In his book Schwartz tells a story of a salesman named Harry, who earned nearly five times as much as the average of all of the other representatives. The sales executive wanted to discover Harry's key to success so he could be used as an example of how to be a better salesman. In reviewing his situation, they discovered that Harry had no particular advantage in education, looks, territory, health, or any other external factor. In short, Harry was about as average a person as the typical American, except for one thing. "The difference between Harry and the rest of the sales force was that Harry thought five times bigger."

In almost every case, David says our limitations are set by the size of our thinking. Americans have proven millions of times over that success is not based on one's situation, circumstances, culture, physical characteristics, or mental capabilities. The amount in your bank account, how happy you are, and how much abundance you have in your life is directly linked to how much you think you <u>can</u> have.

Too often people fail because they believe they are going to fail, not because they don't have the aptitude. William Shakespeare wrote, "There is nothing either good or bad except that thinking makes it so."

> *Whether you believe you can or believe you can't; either way you are right.*
> Henry Ford

Being set free from mediocrity is purely based on your thinking. Inside your body is a "thinking being" and if you haven't done so yet, you need to get acquainted with the real you. You will discover that your ability to improve beyond your current best is based solely on whether you believe you can or whether you believe you can't. Ralph Waldo Emerson said, "Great men [and women] are those who see that thoughts rule the world."

No one enjoys crawling on the ground. We were made to stand erect, walk and then run. Too often our failures are caused by not being able to believe we are capable. In such cases, our failures cannot help us. That is a bad kind of failure and it must be avoided at all costs. In other words, if you don't believe you can, you will fail no matter what your advantages are. The "I'll-give-it-a-try" attitude is not good enough either. It too produces failures.

You need to focus your thinking on believing you-can-do-it." When you say to yourself "I know I can do it," the how-to-do-it develops almost automatically. Jesus said, "All things are possible to him who believes." Belief launches the power to do.

Those who believe they can move mountains; do move mountains. They learn what it takes. They gather the resources. They keep doing whatever is necessary until it happens. Napoleon Hill says the first step to personal achievement is learning that "Whatever you can conceive and believe, you can achieve."

People thought I was crazy when I decided to leave the Coast Guard. But I had a strong belief that shipping companies could operate at a much safer level if they would only break through the glass ceiling of minimum regulatory compliance. I developed a methodology that shows a shipping company how it can actually save money by optimizing their operations so they are safer than what is prescribed by regulations.

Since the Coast Guard cannot require safety measures beyond the regulations, I decided to "retire" and start consulting with shipping companies on my own. I call it "getting on the other side of the rope and pulling it, instead of trying to lead by pushing it around."

When I begin with a company I explain to them that the safety regulations are based upon the minimum requirements that could be agreed upon. Then I show them that, by targeting minimum requirements, they will, by the *Law of Natural Variation*, be operating half the time below the levels that ensure safe operations. When they are operating below the safe level, they are exposed to higher costs of operations and litigation. An example of a ship that was operated at the minimum regulations is the EXXON VALDEZ. It was practically a brand new tanker that met all minimum requirements. But, due to the *Law of Natural Variation*, it went aground. The subsequent oil that was spilled nearly ruined the pristine waters of much of Alaska's coast. The cost to the Exxon Company was well over 6 billion dollars and its still going higher as litigation continues.

However, when a shipping company targets their optimum safety level, then any variation above or below this level will cause a very small variance in operating costs. The chief financial officers of the companies really like that part.

There is one shipping company that is a perfect example of shattering the glass regulatory ceiling. They have used this proactive methodology to design a new class of oil tanker that optimizes safety. The entire design is well above the regulatory minimum requirements. These tankers are of course more expensive. In fact, each tanker will cost nearly twice as much as a "minimum reg" tanker. Still, this proactive company has proven that the cost of operating its new optimized tankers can be easily financed because investors know that business costs won't vary. Within a few short years the company predicts their optimized tankers will be far more profitable than conventional tankers.

> *A person is the product of His own thoughts. Believe BIG. Adjust your thermostat forward.*
> David Schwartz

You can learn a lesson from the proactive company and break the glass ceiling of false expectations. Your own thinking sets your limits. If you want more joy and abundance in your life, then believe that you can have more joy and abundance. Honestly evaluate what is holding you back from really excelling in your life or business. Then find ways to remove those barriers. Start today

with the ones that exist only in your own mind.  You will discover
the key to curing yourself of 'FAILURE-itis.'  I believe you can
and will do it.

- ✓ *Failures can point to where the problems are.  If you optimize
  your life you will have a far greater chance of eliminating the
  failures that keep you from really excelling in life or in
  business.*

- ✓ *If failures stem from your inability to believe you can
  succeed, then decide to stop listening to your negative
  thoughts and only listen to your positive I-can-do-it, I-will-
  do-it thoughts.*

# Strategy 15.

## Failure can be the spice of life, but don't forget to pull the weeds.

If everything you did came out smelling of roses and honeysuckle how boring your life would be. If you achieved everything with minimum effort and it came out exactly as planned, think of how little you would learn. Life would be boring for you. "Do you remember when" is a common phrase when I get together with my brothers and sisters or with my classmates from the Coast Guard Academy. It is funny that it seems to be the failures, problems, lost games, hard times, cuts, broken bones, and the fights that got us into trouble that we seem to remember most fondly. Why do you think that is?

I believe it is because failure is a vitally important spice of life. Some of my best personal memories are of times when I made a big mistake in judgment. I've had some 'bad hair-day' experiences that make me laugh now, but they weren't so funny when they happened. One day I remember was when I had forgotten my shoulder boards for my Coast Guard uniform shirt and actually made it all the way into a meeting with a Captain before it was noticed – how embarrassing! From then on I always rigged my shirt the night before. And, I always have a good laugh when I recall the situation.

My children used to play a lot of games. I noticed that after they got really good at a game it just didn't seem to be fun for them any more and it was completely abandoned. My son, in particular, would play those handheld computer games for hours on end, especially the ones that would increase in complexity as he got better. But once he mastered the whole game, all the way to its highest level of achievement, he would give it away – it had lost its

value.  The emotion of possible failure just wasn't there anymore.
The spice had lost its savor.

> *Adversity is the diamond dust Heaven polishes its jewels with.*
> Leighton

A great many of us like amusement parks, fairs and carnivals.  If you are like me, you've spent a lot of money at them.  Again, they are popular because there are so many challenges in the games and rides of the parks.  The ride designers have probably made a fortune on scaring people half to death, thinking they are going to die one moment and then laughing hysterically the next.

God created an eternity of excitement and we are directly involved in it.   I believe our world was created with the capacity for imperfection for a reason.  God gave us the ability to choose our fate so life would be exciting and He would know who really loved Him.  Since everyone has to choose, no one can fake it.  He could have created us to be the same as the rest of nature, having to obey without question, but that would be boring.  We are not assembly-line creatures.  Each of us is unique, both physically and mentally.

By creating us in His image, yet imperfect, God gave us the ability to learn by trial and error.  All human beings have the capability of thinking and creating either good or evil into existence.  As an example, consider the computer.  It is a twentieth century creation of man.  It was created to be a tool.  Like money, it can be used for either good or bad, depending on who is using it.  It can be used for tremendous benefit, to do our work and make life a lot easier for us.  It adds, subtracts, multiplies, and divides at speeds that most of us can hardly imagine.  It processes our words into electronic pages that can effortlessly be printed out on one or one million pieces of paper.  It helped me to write this book.  It did the formatting, fixed most of my horrific spelling, and even helped me improve my grammar (don't forget I grew up in Hawaii speaking Pidgin English).

However, there are a great number of people who create evil on the computer in the form of "computer viruses."  People create these "bad" little programs; there can be no other explanation.  The viruses are meant to prey on innocent computer systems so they can no longer be useful for good. Now you and I have the challenge of updating the "inoculation" programs that block computer viruses. Because of such programs, my computer, which is about 100 times faster than the one I had 10 years ago, still reacts just as slowly to commands because it is vigilantly checking for harmful viruses and eliminating them before they have a chance to do any damage.

> *Prosperity is too apt to prevent us from examining our conduct; but adversity leads us to think properly of our state, and so is most beneficial to us.*
>
> Johnson

To me, there is no greater example of how man has the capacity for both good and bad. But what does this mean for you and I? It means that we need to remain vigilant to the task of examining ourselves, watching out for destructive traits and characteristics. You and I are like a garden that, if left untended, will produce an abundance of weeds. If our character and behavioral traits are left unchecked, you can be certain that our virtues will not rage out of control. In fact, the opposite is true.

My vegetable garden was a perfect example of what happens when you don't cultivate what you want to grow. For two years it had not produced much because of a severe drought both years. Another dry summer was predicted, so I thought it wasn't worth the effort and didn't plant any vegetable seeds – none. As it turns out, this area of Virginia received some much-needed rain. However, instead of vegetables, the garden was overflowing in weeds – about three feet high. There wasn't a single vegetable plant that I could see. Since I didn't plant the weeds, where did they come from?

It is the natural state of our being that, if not tended, our faults and failures will eventually choke out our good qualities. We must therefore give attention to the garden of our lives, in which our character traits exist. We start by first admitting that bad character traits (weeds) do exist. Then we get busy pulling them out. Do not fret if you can't tell which are the weeds and which are the good vegetables.  Follow the advice that Jesus gave in one of his Biblical parables.  He said, "let them grow side by side for a while; the differences will soon become evident; you will know which are the weeds by the fruit they produce."

In other words, by self-examination, we will be able to see which character traits cause bad things to happen in our lives.  For example, if we allow the character trait of lying to grow, we will soon see the fruit of mistrust grow in our lives.  If we were in business, particularly if we happened to be in sales, our ability to make a living would be severely hampered.  Thus, we would want to deal with lying as soon as possible.

> *He who calls in the aid of an equal understanding doubles his own; and he who profits by a superior understanding raises his powers to a level with the heights of the superior understanding he unites with.*
>
> Burke

Jesus then recommended that when the weeds become evident, you "pull them out and cast them into the fire."  His words are figurative, but the meaning is clear:  get out of the habit of lying.  Of course nature abhors a vacuum, so you need to consider which good character traits are the ones that should be planted in your life.

The Bible has many suggestions.  My favorites are those referred to in Galatians as the fruits of the Spirit:  love, joy, peace, patience, kindness, goodness, faithfulness, gentleness, and self-control.  The character traits recommended in Strategy 2 are also appropriate.  They will help you to have a "ready for success" personality.

I love Jack Canfield and Mark Victor Hansen's *Chicken Soup for the Soul* books.  So many of their stories seem to be aimed at helping people to realize the value of a solid character.  In their *Chicken Soup for the Christian Soul* book, a story is told about a mother who was dying of cancer.  The story brought tears to my eyes, as many of their stories do.  This Christian woman seemed to be very brave and particularly proactive.  During the weeks that preceded her death, she made several cassette tapes filled with motherly advice for her three young girls, ages 6, 4, and 2.

This young godly woman knew she was not going to be around for her daughters during those special character building experiences and she wanted to help as best she could.    She dictated her thoughts about their first day of school, becoming sweet 16, their first date and first kiss, confirmation, etc.  However, the tape that helped the girls the most and that showed them the true love and superior character of their mother was the one that encouraged them to love their new mother.

Here is what she said: "Ruthie, Hannah, and Molly, some day your daddy will bring a new mommy home.  I want you to make her feel very special, and how proud you will make me feel if you are kind, patient and encouraging to her as she learns to take care of each of you.  Help her set the table.  Please bring her dandelions to put in the special vase – most important, hug her often."  It still brings tears to my eyes.

I recommend you identify which characteristics you want to cultivate in your life and make a plan to develop them.  By the *Law of Sowing and Reaping*, if you sow the right character seeds you will reap the right character.  For example, I wanted to be a good parent so I sought the counsel of the master gardener of good parenting, Dr. James Dobson.  My children are proof-positive that this master of pro-family advocacy knows what he is talking about.  Now that I am doing more public speaking, I want to be the best I can possibly be; therefore, I have created an action plan to develop the character traits I need to become an inspirational speaker.  I have found the master gardener of public speaking, Dale Carnegie, to provide the best advice on what to plant.

This methodology of removing the weeds and planting good character traits is exactly what Ben Franklin used when he decided to improve himself.  He tells about it in his autobiography and you can find my list in Strategy 2.  First he decided which character traits he wanted to have and then developed a plan for planting and growing them in his life by systematically focusing on each one for a week.  You would be wise to do the same.

> *Talents are best nurtured in solitude; character is best formed in the stormy billows of the world.*
> Goethe

If you want to be a successful businessperson, then I recommend you seek the advice of master gardeners of business leadership. I have sought the help of many. I have found the best advice from Dan Kennedy, Napoleon Hill, Robert Allen, Brian Tracy, and Peter Lowe.

Be vigilant and proactive; attack your faults when they are detected. Stay awake, be alert to their presence. Your failures will often be the first to point out your faults to you. Failures can be a spice that will make your life more livable. They can also make you the kind of person the rest of us really enjoy being around. Your character is something that can be improved in your life just like anything else. Break away from what other people say you are. Shatter the glass ceiling by determining for yourself the kind of person you want and need to be. Act like the person you want to be and you will become that person. There are no limits except for what you have set for yourself.

✓ *Those events that bring adversity or the opportunity for failure can actually bring fun and excitement to our lives; don't underestimate their value.*

✓ *You determine your own character – not your parents or grandparents, and not your culture. They might be an influence, but the choice is yours.*

✓ *Never give up watching for the weeds that appear in your life. Left untended, they will choke the good character traits and leave you wanting.*

# Strategy 16.

# Become a success by letting others know how you overcame failure.

Some of the most famous people are those who started out either as miserable failures or had to overcome tremendous adversity. They did not have success handed to them; rather, they realized that if they wanted to succeed they would have to take the responsibility for overcoming whatever odds confronted them. Not only did they confront their difficulties, they purposefully used adversity to propel themselves to success. They have taught us that success does indeed lie on the far side of failure.

Thomas Edison was kicked out of school at a young age, educated himself, and then became the greatest inventor of all time. Andrew Carnegie was just a poor immigrant boy whose father died, leaving him with the responsibility of providing for his mother and younger brother. He invested his money, taught himself the railroad and steel business, and then became one of the richest Americans of all time.

*All the world over it is true that a double-minded man is unstable in all his ways, like a wave on the streamlet, tolled hither and thither with every eddy of its tide. A determinate purpose in life and a steady adhesion to it throughout all disadvantages, are indispensable conditions of success.*

W.M. Punshon

Helen Keller was struck deaf, blind, and mute by a childhood disease. Not only did she learn how to communicate brilliantly, she became an author and lecturer and an inspiration to us all. Napoleon Hill was a young back-hills ruffian who was schooled by his stepmother to be a reporter. He learned the value of having a definite major purpose, and then developed the science of personal achievement. Although Franklin

Roosevelt had polio, he learned how to focus intently on his persuasive abilities and then became, in the opinion of many, one of America's greatest Presidents.

You have been learning throughout this book not to be afraid to fail, but rather to manage failure so that it accelerates your learning, helps you to enjoy life more, helps you to have self-confident children, and even helps bring you more peace of mind. Now I want to encourage you even more by pointing out that many people have become wildly successful just by telling other people how they used to be failures (fat, poor, ugly, unhappy, dumb, lonely, addicted, etc.) and then showing us how they overcame their problem.

Robert G. Allen is a guru on 'infopreneuring.' He started out penniless, but learned that he could still buy real estate without any money, which then made him a good bit of money. However, when he wrote his book about it, called *Nothing Down*, he made a fortune and started his infopreneuring empire. Many others have done likewise and created huge information empires by telling others how, through sheer willpower, newfound knowledge, or some special miracle, they overcame failure and now live a life of success. Robert tells how to be an infopreneur in his book *Multiple Streams of Income,* and states "Almost all success books are based on personal failures." Robert Allen also says, "Intellectual property is the real wealth of the new millennium."

I've mentioned Dale Carnegie as one of the most respected teachers on public speaking; yet he tells of how he failed miserably by starting out practicing and teaching what didn't work. His discovery of how to remove the fear of public speaking, a fear that is ranked higher than any other fear, including death, put him on the road to success. For the rest of his life he traveled that road and told his stories of overcoming his failure. He became a true American legacy by being willing to teach others what he learned from his and other peoples' speaking mistakes. Besides leaving us a legacy, he made large sums of money selling his courses and books.

> *When a man has been guilty of any vice or folly, the best atonement he can make for it is to warn others not to fall into the like.*
> Addison

Dan Kennedy has written several great business books, such as *No B.S. Sales Success, No B.S. Business Success,* and *No B.S. Time Management for Entrepreneurs.* They all have heart-warming stories of how he failed at first. Then Dan unloads a truckload of great ideas that he learned from overcoming his problems, mistakes, and failures. He is a good example of how pointing the spotlight on your own problems sometimes makes you more believable in what you say.

There are some companies that have used this idea on product marketing, too. For example, a blemish or so-called "design flaw" became a boon for Volkswagen. Do you remember the VW car advertising of the 1960's? It was as ugly as a bug, which made it all the more popular. It even became known as the VW Beetle and the VW Bug. The faults and idiosyncrasies of the car were made fun and lovable. These failures, rather than being embarrassing to the company, actually gave the car credibility. The VW Bug became a failure-to-success story in its own right.

Another infopreneuring giant is Brian Tracy. As an author, sales trainer, and motivational speaker, he is one of the finest in the world. However, he started out as a high school dropout, working at hard labor types of jobs and sleeping in his car. But he had one redeeming quality; he liked to read. As he read, he began to learn from others how to become successful. He tried putting their ideas into practice. He customized their ideas to fit his own circumstances and they worked. He became a very successful businessman. But he discovered that he had even more success as an author and speaker, sharing his rags-to-riches story. The great thing about this kind of information is that the more of it you give away; the more you benefit others and yourself.

I could go on for pages telling about both men and women who have turned their lives around and are now making a living helping others to overcome the problems of their lives. Many speak and write, and have turned their life stories into wealth by producing such things as books, tape programs, seminars, newsletters, video courses, speeches, consulting practices, and success posters. Their willingness to pass on to us what they have learned has obviously benefited them. But it has also benefited me in ways that I am still discovering as I learn their methods.

Why not give other people a chance to learn from your failures? If it is because you haven't become successful yet, then consider the following question. What would it take to motivate you? Think about it. How have others done it?

If you look at it from a proactive point of view, it is like someone is offering you $50,000 dollars to lose the 50 pounds that you have always wanted to lose. All you have to do is come up with a plan for how to lose it and then be willing to tell others about your own failure-to-success story.

How much is that perfect relationship worth? Paul Hartunian, another infopreneuring champion and Public Relations guru, has made a small fortune by telling people about how he overcame his problem of finding the love of his life. He felt so confident that the solution he found would work for others too, that he wrote all about it in his book, *How to Be Outrageously Successful With the Opposite Sex.* He promises it will "solve every problem you've ever had … meeting, dating or marrying the man or woman of your dreams."

*It is my firm belief that everyone – including you – has at least one good book in them.*
Robert G. Allen

How about that addiction or bad habit that you want to kick? Take that thought to the next step. What if someone offered you 10 million dollars to overcome that fear of failure, which has been holding you back all this time from pursuing the career you've always wanted? You are now in the "before" picture. All you have to do is motivate yourself to step out of the before and into the "after" picture. Don't limit yourself. You can do it if you take control of your mind, set a goal, create a plan, and then take action to achieve it.

Once you motivate yourself to learn whatever it is that will move you into the success arena, then you will have two large benefits. The first benefit is breaking free of mediocrity. You will actively be solving your problem and be much happier with yourself. The second is that it will give you a source of income if you are willing to market your newly discovered know-how. You might not be interested in turning it into an information empire like the people mentioned above, but it could bring in a modest income in a variety of ways.

Nearly everything that is taught and learned follows the same system. My daughter Deborah started out in karate not knowing a thing about it, except for what she had seen in some Jackie Chan movies. She was motivated to learn however, so she found a studio where she could learn from others. Those who taught her seemed to be experts, but she found out that they too started out knowing next to nothing. Now Deborah can teach and those who are learning from her see her as an "expert." She continues her own climb as her level of expertise increases. As long as she is willing to make mistakes and learn from them she will continue to get better. She likes to teach because it reinforces what she has learned, benefits others, and boosts her self-confidence.

*What lies behind us and what lies before us are tiny matters compared to what lies within us.*
Ralph Waldo Emerson

In earlier strategies I spoke of the benefit of learning from the failures of others. Now it is your turn; let others learn from you. How you deal with your failures can be a tremendous inspiration to other people. Perhaps it may even be an eye-opener to someone trapped in mediocrity by circumstances similar to your own. When people see that you are not perfect, yet you persevered, they will have hope and courage. Maybe you will be motivated to become the expert if you knew that other people are desperate for answers and they need you to teach them how to do it.

This book is, in part, my own failure-to-success story. I had been successful as a Coast Guard officer, but I was not living the abundant life I was meant to have until I lost my fear of failure. I was afraid to leave my secure government job until I figured out that, in order to become a real success – one who has peace of mind and other things money can't buy – <u>I needed to do what I was meant to do</u>, no matter the outcome. I learned how to manage my failures and cured myself of FAILURE-itis. You can too, if you follow the strategies that I have learned and now pass on to you. You will learn that the glass ceiling that was above you can be shattered. Do what you were meant to do, learn to break free of mediocrity, and then tell others how you are now SUCCESS BOUND.

✓ *If you haven't broken away from mediocrity yet, look for the motivation to do so. You might think about what others will pay you to teach them. Perhaps you would enjoy helping them overcome their failures.*

✓ *Become an expert so you can increase your self-esteem, build your self-confidence and be able to say to yourself and others – "I did it!"*

✓ *Look for ways to tell your "failure-to-success" story so that you and others benefit from your experiences and newfound knowledge.*

# *Part IV*

# *Free To Live and Love*

*Liberty starts in the mind. In the United States some still live as slaves because they are chained to mediocrity. Proactive thinkers are free to live and love no matter what country they're from.*

**Foreword to Part IV**

As a citizen of the United States, March 4th is also to be celebrated as a Day of Independence, for it honors a rare victory of the intellect. On March 4th, 1789 the Constitution of the United States of America became the supreme law of this great nation. The U.S. Constitution establishes a freedom for individuals that is unequaled, for it not only limits the power of government, which protects us from tyranny, but it also guarantees freedoms to believe and to express our beliefs as we feel is appropriate. The fight to secure the inalienable rights of life, liberty, and the pursuit of happiness would have been in vain, had the U.S. Constitution not completed the act of setting us free in our minds.

There isn't anyone living in the United States of America that should have to live in poverty. Any one who thinks that they or anyone else must succumb to poverty is dead wrong. That type of limited thinking is what causes poverty and takes away peace of mind and happiness.

Success and abundance can be achieved by choosing to think in such a way that your actions produce success and abundance. Being successful does not in any way take from others, any more than choosing to put a smile on your face would take a smile away from another person.

Others do not have to be sad in order for you to be happy. Others do not have to be dumb in order for you to be smart.

Acquiring wealth in response to an opportunity of service to others never takes away from another individual; it just can't happen. I believe the opposite is true. If everyone would pursue success and abundance, by setting themselves free to live and love, then poverty would be eradicated.

The strategies of Part IV are dedicated to helping you become the type of person who enjoys the freedom to think on your own. Make your forefathers happy by using that freedom in the pursuit of your own happiness – be free to live and love.

# Strategy 17.

# Be patient with your failures.

Getting too caught up in the desire for instant everything will not contribute to your success, particularly when it comes to learning from your failures. If you try to fail too fast in order to learn fast, you may lose your self-confidence, self-respect and/or self-esteem. Look around you and notice the car salesman chain smoking on the other side of the showroom. Watch the news and see a promising athlete lose it all to drugs. Read the newspaper and learn about another burned-out executive who just got picked up for drinking while driving.

I have discovered that in order for me to manage the timing of my failures, I have to be patient with learning the lessons that failures and setbacks bring. I have found that it is to my benefit to learn all that I can from each failure – to milk them for all they're worth. You need to have patience and self-discipline in order to let the lesson sink in before rushing on to the next one. Let the lesson have its full effect.

Life is short – BUT IT'S NOT THAT SHORT. Learn to be patient with the timing of your failures and your aptitude for learning from them. Don't push yourself too fast. Move on when you are ready and set realistic goals. This is an important lesson to learn. If you are not patient and you move too quickly, it will be like trying to hurry along the eating and digestive process.

> *Haste is not always speed. We must learn to work and wait. This is like God, who perfects his works through beautiful graduations.*
> Moliere

Our American society is now filled with all sorts of fast food restaurants. They are all designed to reduce the amount of time between ordering a meal and eating it; it is now just a matter of moments. But if you eat your food as fast as it was served, instead of enjoying the meal and getting nourishment, you will only get an upset stomach and lengthen the digestive process.    You will feel ill rather than energized.

Michael Gelb, in his book, *How To Think Like Leonardo da Vinci*, tells us what the great genius painter thought about eating.  "... shun wantonness, and pay attention to diet, ... eat only when you want and sup light, ... eat simple food, ... chew well, ..." This is good advice to follow for eating and for learning from failures. Since this great genius believed in balance, he probably would have told you that it was important to accept personal responsibility for your health and well-being, both physically and psychologically.

I have also discovered that learning from failures is similar to praying, in that it takes patience.  It seems that many of the great geniuses of the past believed that there is a lesson to be learned from each and every situation, but it is not always obvious and it can't be rushed.

Just like praying, the lessons that come from failures sometimes take longer than you might think is necessary.  Robert Schuller, preacher, motivational speaker and author of *Be (Happy) Attitudes*, teaches "God's delays are not necessarily God's denials."  If you pray for something and it doesn't work, don't fret, just keep on praying.  The same applies to learning from failures; the lesson will come at the right time.  Keep on expecting to learn and improve and you will.

If you do not improve at the rate you expect, then try to figure out why.  Sometimes you do not get what you ask for because you don't really believe in what you are asking for.  The Bible also says, "as you believe, so shall you receive."  By the *Law of Belief*, you can only get what you truly believe in.  Therefore, whatever you ask for must be in alignment with your firmly held beliefs or it will not happen.  In the Bible it says, "... let him ask in faith, without wavering, for a double-minded man is unstable in all his ways." The same could be said about faith in learning through your failures.

> *Whatever your mind can conceive and believe, you can achieve.*
>
> Napoleon Hill

I have experienced times when the lesson that should have come from a failure was not readily apparent. It was not until I analyzed my belief system that I discovered I wasn't ready for the lesson. What and how you believe is determined by your mind, which in a very large measure determines the joy and abundance that you receive in your life.

The person who helped me the most with learning how beliefs can affect success is Tony Robbins. In his book, *Unlimited Power*, Tony outlines seven beliefs that he says are commonly held among the successful people that he has studied. I paraphrase them below as I have understood them and incorporated them into my belief system. If you find that you do not yet hold to these beliefs, then I highly recommend you consider adding them to your belief system. I feel confident that you will enjoy the same success that I have had, you will more easily and quickly learn the lessons that are meant to come from your failures.

Belief 1 – Everything happens for a definite purpose and it works out in my best interest. I was recently in a museum dedicated to the Confederate General Thomas "Stonewall" Jackson, a committed Christian army officer. On one of the plaques it quoted his favorite Bible verse, taken from the Book of Romans "God causes all things to work together for good, for those who love God and are called according to His purpose." When you do the work that you were meant to do you can be certain that everything is already worked out for your benefit.

There are many different ways to react to any given situation. If you choose to react in such a way as to expect that good will come of it, then you are sure to learn the requisite lesson. Start believing that everything is happening to serve you and you will find it easier to discipline yourself to react to a negative situation in a positive way. It will help you to retrace your steps mentally and do what must be done to mend fences and rebuild relationships. I have found that it also helps me to be thankful that things were not worse than they were and to take responsibility for looking at the new possibilities that have sprung up.

**Belief 2 – I am never a failure, but a person who successfully achieves results each time I try until I get the outcome I desire.** This is similar to the first belief, but adds a positive emphasis on learning how to make adjustments and to keep on trying, again and again, until you succeed. It will help you to rid yourself of the fear of failure. It will open your eyes to the fact that the most successful people have been those who have learned what went wrong, made adjustments, and then tried again. This belief has taught me to hope that I can succeed at whatever I've put my mind to.

> *Seeing much, suffering much, and studying much, are the three pillars of learning.*
> Disraeli

I am sure that you can think of times when you have not gotten what you wanted. It could have been missing an 'A' in a class, losing a contract despite a promising business proposal, or ending a relationship just when you were really beginning to feel good about it. Belief number two will help you realize that failures are disappointing results that indicate you have a little more to learn. You must understand that each attempt you make will give you experience, which is an asset you can obtain only by living each day as it comes.

Mark Twain said, "There is no sadder sight than a young pessimist, his belief almost guarantees a mediocre existence." Tony Robbins says, "Winners, leaders, masters – people with personal power – all understand that if you try something and do not get the outcome you want, it is simply feedback." Do not let yourself believe that you are a failure, not in the slightest. When results are disappointing, let the positive emotion of faith in your major purpose keep you focused on learning what you can, so you will keep moving forward.

<u>Belief 3 – I am responsible for everything that happens.</u>  I have come to understand the *Law of Correspondence*, which says that our outer world will correspond to the thoughts and feelings of our inner world.  You can create new circumstances around you by being responsible for what you think about.  In fact, you are the only one who can be responsible for what you think so you are the only person who can be responsible for your circumstance.

I had a difficult time with this belief because of some conflicting ideas heard in some sermons a long time ago.  But the research I did on my own, both from the Bible and from other very successful and influential businessmen and scholars, confirmed that I was the creative force in my world.  You and I have been formed in God's image and given the same creative nature.  As human beings, we are the only part of nature that can determine our own habits; all other creatures and all other physical elements have fixed habits.

> *The key to every man is his thought. Sturdy and defying though he look, he has a helm which he obeys, which is the idea after which all his facts are classified.  He can only be reformed by showing him a new idea which commands his own.*
>
> Ralph Waldo Emerson

You have within you the potential for greatness <u>and</u> for mediocrity; they are both an innate part of your character.  It is your choice as to whether you lift up your eyes and look to the unlimited possibilities, or mope about looking for an easy life somewhere around that next elusive corner.  What you think about most will eventually become your reality.  If you constantly worry about money, then money problems will inhabit your life.  On the other hand, if you find ways to approach every problem with hope, as if you can control your circumstances, you will find ways to make yourself very valuable and will be compensated accordingly.

<u>Belief 4 – I do not have to understand everything, I just need a basic knowledge of how to use the tools I have acquired.</u>  This world is becoming more and more complicated.  For Thomas Edison, creating the light bulb was really advanced science.  Now

it is *simple*, even for a young grade-school student. The good thing is that most of what is being invented does not require that we have a complete understanding of all of the theory behind it in order to use it.

While getting my Masters degree in naval architecture I took several advanced electives in computer design. The personal computer had just been invented and I wanted to know how they could be used for ship design. When I graduated I could design simple computers and program in all of the known computer languages at that time. However, I discovered that it was impossible to keep up with all of the changes that rapidly took place in the following 10 years. It was a major breakthrough for me to incorporate the 4$^{th}$ belief and not fret over having to understand everything about a computer in order to use it. All I needed was the basic understanding of the software interfaces.

If asked, would you be able to explain how a computer works or how a word-processing program functions? Probably not and you probably don't care that you don't. But that doesn't mean that you can't use one effectively. Similarly, you can learn the tools that are associated with the universal laws that I have been talking about without having to understand exactly how they work. Just accept that they do and learn how to use them effectively as tools.

<u>Belief 5 – I need the help and cooperation of other people to become truly successful in life.</u> The most obvious example of this to me is my extraordinarily capable wife Cathy. I sometimes think that if you were to look next to the word "helpmate" in the dictionary that you would see her picture. From having children, to educating them, to being the ideal officer's wife, to running a business, and now to being editor of books and course material – I could NOT have done it without her.

> *No man is an island unto himself.*
> Old adage

Even the most brilliant of persons needs to work with others to have his or her idea come to fruition. Long lasting success can only be achieved by having rapport with those with whom you have a co-dependent relationship.

Not just the employees that work for you, but a network of people that you can draw from and vice versa.

I've learned that all good relationships are built on trust and respect and high levels of cooperation. If you do not have those character traits then I recommend that you work on acquiring them so that you can build your network. For superlative advice on how to network I recommend reading Harvey Mackay's book, *Dig Your Well Before You're Thirsty.*

If you want to have lasting success, then you will need to incorporate this belief of co-dependency with others into your thinking process and then go to work at acquiring the people skills that you will need to have to establish and maintain good relationships. There are a lot of books available on how to have good relationships. The all-time best business book on the subject is Dale Carnegie's *How to Win Friends & Influence People.* If you have not yet read it, I highly recommend it.

Belief 6 – The work I do is fun and exciting because I am doing what I am meant to do. It almost seems too good to be true. Am I really supposed to have fun doing what I am meant to do? The answer is an emphatic YES! No one has ever been known to have long lasting success at doing what he or she hates or simply puts up with. I believe that part of the reason this is true is because it takes enthusiasm and passion to get good at what you do, and you don't get those emotions from doing what is dull, dreary, or boring.

I believe that the true secret in living a great life is finding an occupation that you would do even if you didn't get paid for it. Mark Twain said, "The secret of success is making your vocation your vacation." I've also heard it said that you know that you have found your life's work when you can't imagine ever retiring from it. I now feel that way about my work helping people and organizations achieve more success through proactive thinking. Proactive thinking not only has uses beyond measure in the maritime industry, but it is useful and applicable in all aspects of life; personal, business, social, political, educational, selling, parenting, leading, etc. – there is no limit to its potential for serving people.

If you have a hard time with this belief, then I recommend you read Mark Albion's book, *Making a Life – Making a Living: Reclaiming Your Purpose and Passion in Business and in Life.* This book is too new to have been responsible for the changes that I made in my life, but I would gladly provide a testimonial to its truth and value.

<u>Belief 7 – I am committed to my mission; it will bring me abiding success, happiness, and peace of mind.</u> Tony Robbins says it very powerfully "There is no great success without great commitment." The Bible looks at it from a different point of view; "the man who puts his hand to the plow and then looks back is not worthy of the kingdom of heaven." I have observed that having a burning desire to achieve an objective is far more valuable than any other attribute, including brains, talent, good looks, physical strength, and agility.

> *Self-responsibility is the core quality of the fully mature, fully functioning, self-actualizing individual.*
> Brian Tracy

When I was in the Eighth Grade, I had a strong desire to attend college, but my father told me that when I reached eighteen, I would be on my own. As happens when you set your mind to achieving a goal, I learned about U.S. military service academies from a family friend. He told me that they were free <u>and</u> the service paid you while you attended. That's what I wanted. He realized how serious I was and helped me to completely plan out my high school years, so that when the time came I would be in a good position to be selected.

I committed myself to the plan, taking all of the right classes, playing on several sports teams, joining and taking leadership roles in organizations, etc. It wasn't easy, but I believed in the plan. There were many, many days when I was gone from 6 a.m. until 10 p.m. It was no surprise to me that I was the first 'Maui Boy' to be selected to attend the U.S. Coast Guard Academy. It was a scholarship worth about $80,000 at that time. I believe that the plan paid off, not because I was talented in any special way, but because I was committed to my goal.

When Brian Tracy talks about purpose, he puts the emphasis on clarity. To be successful, he says you need to "be absolutely crystal clear about what you want." Al Ries in his book, *Focus: The Future of Your Company Depends On It*, puts the emphasis on knowing and sticking to the niche of where you are the best at serving your customer. It all comes down to the same thing. You will find that you will get more of what you want in life if you are committed to doing what you are meant to do. Don't get sidetracked with what appears to you to be the necessities of life. Stay focused, be clear about your purpose in life, and be committed.

You do not need to look far to see lives that are affected by moving too quickly without learning from failures: burnout, unhappiness, substance abuse, etc. Early signs of moving off course from your purpose in life are that you begin to feel inadequate and you encounter strained relationships. You lose your enthusiasm and creativity and then you start to lose your ability to bounce back after you experience some type of adversity or failure.

> *If we don't change our direction, we are likely to end up where we are headed.*
> An old Chinese Proverb

If you begin to notice these signs in yourself, intentionally slow things down so you can refocus, recharge, and redirect. All learning takes time and you won't always make progress at the same rate, in fact it you will nearly always have fluctuations. All through your life you will hit plateaus in your learning, just like there were spurts and plateaus in your physical growth. Just keep on, keeping on. There is an old saying, "Unreasonable haste is the direct road to error."

You will enjoy far more happiness and peace of mind if you learn to live with the rhythms that nature has established for you.

Everything has a rhythm.   Our minds are no different.   For example, if we are impatient with our sleep patterns and try to "burn the candle at both ends," we usually end up suffering in some way.   When you are patient with your physical and psychological needs and work with them, you will be able to overcome the struggles and failures you face.   When you have a high level of self-confidence and self-esteem you will be able to really live and love to your heart's content.

✓ *Have patience with your learning process.  If you push yourself to learn too quickly your mind and possibly your body will start to rebel.*

✓ *Review your belief systems.  Make sure that you have the beliefs that will ultimately lead to your success and will help you to learn better and more quickly.*

# Strategy 18.

# If you want your children to succeed, let them fail.

My wife and I were the same as all young parents; we wanted our children to grow up healthy and to be successful. We read several books about raising children and we talked to other parents. We asked, "How do you let a child learn by experience yet not get burned?" We wanted our children to learn from experience but we also wanted them to be safe. We soon realized that it was a difficult question and even seasoned parents were just as puzzled as we were.

> *A smooth sea never made a skillful mariner, neither do uninterrupted prosperity and success qualify for usefulness and happiness. The storms of adversity, like those of the ocean, rouse the faculties, and excite the invention, prudence, skill, and fortitude of the voyager.*
>
> Unknown

As in most aspects of parenting, answers to these kinds of questions are not easy. Of course we received a fair amount of advice, some that worked, some that didn't. The following is the tried and true advice that we pass on to others. It is based on our own experience raising our three children and sharing the responsibility for many other children through church and youth organizations. The advice is in three parts:

1. Don't let life be too easy on your children,
2. Let them have the chance to fail on their own once in a while, and
3. Pray to God for mercy.

This is sound advice for all parents, teachers, and youth leaders. If you are too easy on your children you may be stealing their future successes from them.

In his book, *Think & Grow Rich*, Napoleon Hill told of his humble beginnings and how it helped him to prepare for the future. He told of how he was purposely named after a rich uncle in hopes that his family might receive some portion of an inheritance. Hill says that his entire side of the family was left out of the will and it was probably the best thing that ever happened to him. He says that without hardship he might have wound up doing "nothing" just like the rest of the family who did receive the money. But as it turned out, adversity taught him to work hard which, when the right time came along, set him up to be challenged by Andrew Carnegie to develop the science of personal achievement.

Most parents have the tendency to be protective and give their children all that they can. It is a natural tendency for parents to want their children to have a fun-filled and easy life. After all, who doesn't want their child to have it better that they did? But, like everything else in life, you need to strike a balance in order to seek an optimum performance. It is especially "dangerous" to give too many good things to your children without them earning those good things. Do not preclude them from learning the hard way.

> *You're going to make mistakes. The key is to learn from them as fast as possible, and make changes as soon as you can. That's not always easy to do because ego and pride get in the way, but you have to put all that aside and look at the big picture.*
>
> Tiger Woods

We wanted to raise our children to think for themselves, learn from their mistakes, and be able to persevere when confronted with adversity. We discovered that self-confidence – the trust in one's own ability – is a key ingredient to success in life. To build up their self-confidence they need to have successful experiences of overcoming their inadequacies and learning how to improve. I believe that it is necessary to start off by arranging small successes. You do this by breaking tasks down into easily managed and simple components, ones they can understand and master.

My wife Cathy grew up as the second oldest in a large family and learned how to cook and be responsible for preparing meals. When she got to college she was in a co-op dormitory in which the girls all took turns making the meals. Cathy was amazed at how many of the girls had never learned how to cook; some had never even made desserts. Their parents had been too easy on them and actually robbed them of the joy of cooking. Cathy took the time to teach them how to cook and she vowed that her children would learn how to cook at an early age. By the time our children were high school age, they did nearly all of the menu planning, shopping and cooking and Cathy and I enjoyed time together doing the dishes after the supper meal.

One of the shortcomings I've observed in our modern school systems is when teachers tend to shield children from failure for most of the school year, until the BIG failure of flunking a class comes crashing down at the end. Children are sheltered too much from adverse consequences during the school year. The system doesn't allow children to form a strong mental relationship between controlling the learning experience and reaping the rewards of improvement. For example, if a child fails a class in the first six-week marking period, what are the consequences? Typically, there are no consequences until the end of the school year (if at all), and there is often no connection with the "failure" and no opportunity for really learning the material. I believe that sheltering children from experiencing the right level of failure, condemns them to lives of mediocrity and possibly sets them up to lose their self-esteem when they fail at life's real lessons.

Nothing builds up a child's self-esteem better than unconditional love. Make sure your children know that you love them for who they are, and not just for what they do to please you. If you love your children, teach them to believe they are never failures, even though they make mistakes or encounter difficulties from time to time.  When you discipline, it is always their behavior you are upset with, not your children.  Teach them how to learn from the adversity of your discipline.

It is hard to watch your child fail at something, but you must encourage little Johnny to walk on his own and let him suffer the requisite falls.  Be encouraging and patient as your children push their comfort zone out in other areas of life as well.  Tell them "You can do it; just keep trying."  Then reward them for their efforts as well as their accomplishments.

Another important lesson is to teach them how to fairly evaluate themselves.  Treat all mistakes as good learning opportunities.  Let them see that you make mistakes and that you learn from them too.  Give children gentle and accurate feedback when they fall short of expectations and then lead them forward with your enthusiastic encouragement.    Giving   inaccurate   feedback   of  children's performance, like saying, 'you did a great job' when they really didn't, might seem like a form of encouragement, but it is not.  The only way to build genuine self-esteem is to respect your children's ability to learn by giving accurate truthful feedback that will help them improve.

I found that it was important to challenge my children in ways that taught them to love challenges.   Together we read a lot of adventure stories, and my wife and I helped them to write and produce their own plays.  We helped them to push themselves in ways that stretched their imaginations as well as abilities.

*In the final analysis, it is not what you do for your children, but what you have taught them to do for themselves that will make them successful human beings.*

Ann Landers

Have you ever read a good story that had no adversity, no conflict, or no setbacks?  No, of course not.  So make it a habit to read to your children and help them to love to read themselves.  Even in fictional books, where anything is possible and heroes may spring full-grown, the favorite heroes are the ones who started out very naïve.  They bumbled their way from challenges into terrible messes – messes that they often needed help to get out of. The reader is then given the chance to participate in the learning and growing process that makes the hero great in the end.

Heroes need to be developed. There can be no hero without a victory first. And there is no victory without the possibility of failing at something important. Let your children be heroes. Give them a chance and they might teach you a thing or two about what makes heroes lovable. You will never be the perfect parent and you most likely will never have perfect children. But you will have the necessary ingredients for the rich rewards of living and loving as you learn how to manage your failures together.

✓ *Children want and need challenges. Give them opportunities that will help them to mature into healthy young adults with lots of self-confidence and self-esteem.*

✓ *Teach your children not to be afraid of failure but to use it as their teacher. Allow your children to be heroes.*

*Don't be afraid to fail. Don't waste energy trying to cover up failure. Learn from your failures and go on to the next challenge. It's OK to fail. If you're not failing, you're not growing.*

H. Stanley Judd

# Strategy 19.

## Forgive yourself for your failures.

Suicide is never the answer to any question. The news media is filled with stories of people who have not been able to handle their failures and decided to end it all quickly. It is so prevalent nowadays that most of us probably personally know a family impacted by someone who has 'opted out'. If you know someone who has contemplated suicide, or if you have ever thought about it yourself, this is an important strategy for you.

Suicide is triggered by a low self-esteem. Self-esteem is a fragile thing. Guard it well and protect it through your failures; it will save your life. I believe that it is the power of forgiveness that helps us to maintain our self-esteem throughout the trials of life. I have learned that when intentions are honorable and good, <u>all failures</u> can be forgiven – others and my own.

> *Your friends may come and go, but your enemies accumulate; therefore it's best not to have any.*
> Anonymous

Studies have shown that successful people believe that they are responsible for what happens to them in life; therefore, they find a way to forgive others <u>and</u> themselves. Incorporating the virtue of being responsible for forgiving all mistakes should be a goal of yours.

The *Law of Forgiveness* is a universal law of both the mental and spiritual worlds. This law says that you will be forgiven to the extent that you forgive others. This is a critical law to your ultimate success because it will give you the ability to be in complete control of your mind. Guilt can be crippling. By practicing forgiveness you will be able to proactively set up a barrier against the negative emotion of guilt.

Without forgiveness, guilt accumulates, whether we realize it or not. When problems come up you may experience a bit of guilt. Strong negative emotions can be associated with guilt; they can be interfere with your plans for success. Dan Kennedy warns us to be careful not to confuse taking on responsibility with taking on guilt. He says, "Guilt is warranted only if your intentions were dishonorable." Therefore proactively deal with guilt by making sure all of your intentions are good and right.

Henry Ford, of Ford Motor Company; Tom Monaghan of Dominos Pizza, and Soichiro Honda, founder of Honda Corporation, are just a few of the great businessmen who went bankrupt several times before they finally launched into the outer stratosphere of success. If they had blamed themselves and felt guilty for their first business failures, it is very likely that they would not have had the tenacity to start over again.

If your business goes bust for whatever reason and you have to turn long-time trusted employees out, don't feel guilty. If you did what you could they will understand. Make sure you are not asking them to pay for your financial failure unless they were also receiving part of the opportunity of ownership.

> *As far as the east is from the west; so far has He removed our transgressions from us.*
> King David

Jesus was asked by His disciples, "How many times should we forgive – seven times?" Seven was more than twice the three required by the Law. Jesus answered, "No – you should forgive at least seven times seventy." I believe 490 was a symbolically huge number to them; it was like saying "You must forgive every time." Forgiving others is a very cleansing feeling. It is a feeling that is very close to love. Make a habit of forgiving and you will have a happiness bank account that will be full to overflowing.

The ability to forgive is based on the belief that what has happened in the past is not important – it is what you are going to do in the future that counts. What is important is that you learn from the past so that it does not need to repeat itself. As the old adage goes, those who refuse to learn from history are doomed to repeat it.

Make it a practice to review your performance objectively. If you have fallen short of expectations, ask yourself, "Is there anything I could have done to change the outcome?" If the answer is 'No,' then don't waste any more time worrying about the past. Keep moving forward.

You should always find a way to forgive yourself when you have made a mistake or failed to achieve a goal. We live in a competitive world in which there are winners and losers. In much of life, success is measured only in terms of winning. However, it is not true that victory for one creates a loss of equal proportion for another. A forgiving person is able to create win-win situations almost every time.

Particularly in any type of a business or negotiation endeavor, if both parties do not come out feeling that they have gotten what they wanted, then both parties have lost. Even for the party that may have come out getting more than its fair share, it will have lost the trust of the other. The loss of a reputation for being fair is a serious matter because it is the true long-term measure of business success.

Microsoft is a company that continues to act like a new company. It grows every year at a "start up" company growth rate. I believe that one of the reasons is because they have made "trial and error" acceptable throughout the whole company. They realize a huge profit every year because they are not afraid to let their employees make mistakes. They are willing to take the risk in order to let them learn how to develop software that will make customers really pleased with their products. We all know that they don't always succeed at that, but we can trust that they are always learning from their mistakes and correcting the problems.

If someone has been unhappy with your products or service you may have considered that a failure. But now you know that you don't need to feel that way. In fact, Michael LeBoeuf, in *How to Win Customers and Keep Them for Life,* tells us that statistics provide a very positive message. They indicate that customers who have had problems, which have been corrected, become far more loyal and less apt to switch to a competitor than customers who have always received service without reason to complain.

> *A wise man will make haste to forgive, because he knows the full value of time and will not suffer it to pass away in un-necessary pain.*
>
> Rambler

Work to rid yourself of the feeling of having to be perfect when you launch into a project. That type of fear will drive you away from those who want to help you accomplish your goals. It even drives you away from God. It says in the Bible that He has provided perfection, so that we can be confident that we have become "good enough" in every way. God says in the Book of Isaiah, "Come and let us reason together, though your sins be as scarlet, I will make them as white as wool."

It is OK to strive to be perfect, but accept that you will make mistakes along the way. God says "be perfect as I am perfect" and also "work out your own salvation." I take those together to mean that I should keep working at getting better, but I will let God be my perfection. It is recorded in the Book of the Chronicles that God said to Joshua, "I the Lord am with you, if you are with Me; so take courage, be strong and succeed."

You will succeed, not because you are perfect, but because you are doing what God wants you to do. God is like other parents in that He wants us to succeed. I lead an adult Sunday School class at our church, and I am always amazed at the joy of discovery in grown men or women when they realize how much God is like themselves in His love for us. God does all of the things a good parent does. It's no wonder Jesus taught us to pray, "Our Father, who art in heaven…"

As a father, I feel a tremendous joy when my children do the things asked of them because they want to please me. I don't recall them ever being perfect and I don't think I could love them any more if they were. In fact, I found that as they have moved to the end of their teenage years, I probably make more mistakes in loving them than they do me. It is a good thing that we have all learned how to forgive each other no matter what the situation.

When someone doesn't forgive another person, they become bitter and obsessed with the past. They tie up their futures with schemes of revenge and they squander the richness of the present moment through lack of appreciation.

When people don't forgive themselves, these feelings of bitterness are all internalized. They punish themselves and hold back from their potential, thus setting up for a future that they will not enjoy. They are their own enemies. Their inner thoughts hold only criticism and mockery rather than encouragement.

> *A brave man thinks no one his superior who does him an injury, for he has it then in his power to make himself superior to the other by forgiving it. For to err is human; to forgive, divine.*
> Pope

Failure and defeat are never disgraceful if you have done your best. The only competition that really matters in the long run is the one in which you compete with yourself. You will become more sure of your own talents as they are tested by the fire of adversity. The more you like yourself, the more sure you are of your talents, the easier it is to forgive yourself of your faults, and the higher your self-esteem will be. This is an upward spiral that you should continually strive for. Make it a practice each day to forgive yourself and say out loud "I like myself" – "I forgive myself of any shortcomings" – "I am responsible."

Forgiveness is powerful medicine. It can heal the broken-hearted and bind up the wounds of the afflicted. Don't underestimate the power it has in bringing you peace of mind. In the Bible it is recorded how Jesus taught his disciples to pray. Many people repeat *The Lord's Prayer* regularly. In that prayer we are taught to say, "… forgive us our trespasses, as we forgive those who trespass against us." However, few people remember the very next words of Jesus after teaching that prayer doubly emphasized the need to forgive. He said, "If you forgive men their transgressions, your heavenly Father will also forgive you. But, if you do not forgive men, then your Father will not forgive your transgressions." Shortly after that Jesus also said, "Do not judge, lest you be judged yourself. For in the way you judge, you will be judged; and by your same standard measure, it shall be measured to you."

When you approach mistakes as problems that can bring an equivalent opportunity, as was recommended earlier in the book, forgiveness is easier. You might even have an excitement for forgiving knowing something good awaits you. You will let yourself be free to really live and love the way God had intended all along.

✓ *Guard your self-esteem well and protect it by forgiving yourself for your failures.*

✓ *Learn how to forgive yourself and others. Be true in your intent and your mistakes will not cause you disgrace or guilt.*

# *Strategy 20.*

# *Build trust so you can "Fail In Love"*

Without love and acceptance people have a difficult time with taking on the risk of failing. If trust in a relationship and a genuine appreciation for the other person is lacking, it is very difficult to build support for one another. Therefore trust is a key ingredient for learning from failures, which will eventually lead to your success and the success of those who are close to you.

My wife and I have some married friends who shared an experience with us that seems funny to them now, but I am sure it was very difficult when it happened. The husband grew up in the U.S. and spoke broken Spanish. His wife was from Spain and was just learning to speak English when they met. While getting to know each other, they visited her family in Barcelona and experienced an awful situation. In an effort to compliment her mother's cooking, he tried out his novice Spanish. However, instead of saying the intended "You are a good cook," he pronounced a word incorrectly and said, "You are a good pig." Oh, what a slap he got! If it had not been for a large amount of trust that had already been built up, our friends might very well have ended their relationship right there. But love _and_ trust prevailed and a lesson was learned from failure.

> *To be trusted is a greater compliment than to be loved.*
> J. MacDonald

The telling of that story was actually sparked by another mis-understanding that my daughter Michelle had triggered. Our friends were over for a special dinner. During the dinner there was a blessing "toast" made. Soon after the toast, Michelle, who liked this new experience, lifted her glass and said, "more toast, more toast." Our friend was shocked by Michelle's words and seemed offended.

Fortunately her husband realized that what Michelle was saying, sounded in Spanish like "Death! Death!" He explained that Michelle was just asking for another blessing. In addition to triggering the above story, this little scene taught us all a good lesson – don't judge a person's words or actions too quickly until you are sure of their meaning, especially when different languages or cultures are involved.

I coined the phrase "fail in love" to emphasize that we fail best when we have relationships that are based on love, trust, and mutual respect. If you are in a family where the members love each other very much, you can say or do just about anything without injuring the relationship. Even when serious problems arise or mistakes are made, because of trust, the lines of communication stay open and misunderstandings can be swiftly corrected. This is a fortunate situation that you should try to have – it is a wonderful safety net.

I have observed that where there is a lack of trust, marriages are on very shaky ground. When there is a lack of trust, failure can leave you exposed and vulnerable. Therefore most people attempt to either hide their faults or refuse to try anything new, lest they make a mistake that might cause their fragile relationship to break apart. If you want to have a good relationship you've got to be open to instruction. Further more, you need to be able to instruct or the other person won't know what you like or don't like. Said a different way, you cannot have a good relationship if failures (misunderstandings, mistakes, shortcomings, etc.) are not allowed. This applies even more so when children are involved.

When my wife and I disciplined our children for misbehaving, we were following through in the natural order of things so that our children would learn to obey and have a sense of right and wrong. I believe that it is very important to do this early because children remember the lesson but they do not recall the disciplining. Therefore, those are the best years to teach your children how to obey and how to recognize right from wrong.

I have read and observed that there are several formative stages that children go through during their first four or five years, and it is critical that children learn to trust their parents and acquire a full measure of self-esteem through each stage. My wife and I learned that there was a particular pattern to disciplining that worked best to ensure our children's level of love and trust actually increased, rather than decreased as each of them went through their formative years. The following is the pattern of discipline that we used. There are five necessary elements.

> *Born perfectionists, kids don't like to be reminded that they are products of the Fall. They often think they have the power to avoid making mistakes or failing. Your child needs to learn to grieve his lost perfection, accept his failures, learn from them, and grow. Growing up leaves no other option.*
>
> Dr. Henry Cloud &
> Dr. John Townsend

Recognition of what went wrong. For young children, this element of discipline usually has to be pointed out to them. I believe in being <u>very specific</u>. Even if it is a matter of disobedience, where they feel that what you say doesn't matter, they need to be told that it is wrong to act that way. You must be careful to not make everything a 'no-no.' One of the signs of this happening is hearing a child walking around saying "no, no, no." Our little two year old nephew came back from Germany saying, "Nein, nein, nein." 'No' engenders a negative feeling that turns up later in life as: "I can't do it." "I'm not good enough." I'm not smart enough." etc. Make sure the boundaries between what is right and wrong are clear – <u>don't just say no</u>.

<u>Feeling the full effects of punishment.</u> This element is probably a delicate subject for most parents, but the purpose is to get the attention of the child so he or she associates misbehaving with a negative reward. I believe that it is important to learn appropriate methods for administering punishment. My wife and I tried to make punishment a private thing with each of our children. To facilitate privacy we often administered punishment in the bathroom, because even in public we could ask "do we need to

visit the bathroom" and our message would remain private. When the children were young we had a wooden spoon for each with a sad face drawn on it. Sometimes behavior modification took place just by rattling the spoon drawer. If punishment is administered correctly, the lesson will be remembered, but never the pain, as significant as it may be at the time. When our children were old enough to reach the 'age of reason' (and remembering), we gave them each their spoon as a keepsake – we didn't need it anymore.

<u>Repentance and deciding not to do it again.</u>  This element sometimes took some coaching, but it has a very important objective. The goal is to

> *No discipline seems pleasant at the time, but painful. Later on, however, it produces a harvest of righteousness and peace for those who have been trained by it.*
> Saint Paul

get the children to decide that they are going to try not to repeat the offensive behavior. This is a crucial element of the learning experience. If this step is left out, you and your children will experience the same problems over and over again. Also, if true repentance isn't felt, the lack of taking responsibility may show up later in the children's lives. This is often manifested as a high level of stress and frustration because of a belief that they can't change. A child may be feeling "I will always be the same; there is no point in trying." The same is true for adults and such people fear taking responsibility for problems.

<u>Restitution by correcting the problem or creating the mechanism to keep it from happening again.</u>  I believe that this element taught our children how to solve problems on their own. If a toy was taken away, then the obvious restitution was to give it back. However, there were other problems that took a good bit more creativity, like how do you replace a valuable vase that was broken due to a ball being played with in the living room rather than outside? Although the broken vase was an accident, responsibility must be taken for the behavior that was the root cause of the accident. Restitution seems to be the element most often left out by parents. Not dealing with restitution engenders the notion that you can get away with something as long as you don't get caught or you can claim it was an accident, therefore it was not your fault.

People often fail to realize that the *Law of Compensation* will equalize everything eventually. Please love your children enough to help them take responsibility for ALL of their actions.

<u>Full reestablishment of love, self-esteem, and trust.</u>   There is nothing more important than to make sure that children know they are loved unconditionally. Your love is based on the children being lovable human beings, not on the children having good behavior. My wife and I always tried to let our children know that we wanted them to succeed. However, if they didn't succeed, we still loved them just as much and we would help them learn their lessons. We also strongly believed in helping them retain their self-esteem. We told them how smart they were, how pretty or handsome they were, and how they could do anything that they set their minds to do. We tried to help them each feel proud that they could learn how to follow the rules.

Leave out any one of these elements and discipline will not achieve its objective of helping children to learn from their mistakes. When the act of disciplining is not administered well and with love during the early years, or when children have to be disciplined for bad behavior after the age of five or six, they will start to recall the pain of punishment, rather than just the lesson learned.

> *Train up a child in the way he should go and when he is old he will not depart from it.*
> King Solomon

People who abhor correction display anger and hurt, rather than a willingness to learn, grow, and change. I believe it causes a strong fear of failure later in life, which leads to a life of mediocrity. It is far better for children to learn how to be obedient early on so that for the rest of their lives they can learn lessons naturally by trial and error, which is usually quicker and better.

I recommend that you build up love and trust in your relationships, especially with your family. You will find that you feel much safer in trying new things and stretching your comfort zone.

By the *Law of Attraction*, love attracts love. You cannot receive true love unless you are first willing to give it. Love always involves some risk. Sometimes it involves the tough love of disciplining our children. But it is well worth the effort. Extend your love to others in unqualified, generous, understanding ways and you will have the greatest success in it being received and returned in full measure. Extending love is a way of saying that you want the best for another person, which is a wonderful gift to have returned to yourself.

When you fail at something and have learned a lesson, don't dwell on remembering the punishment. After you have learned the lesson, fill your mind with positive thoughts and look forward to what you can do with the new understanding to help yourself, your family, and your friends. This is a sure formula for success, happiness, and peace of mind. This is how you really learn to live and love.

✓ *Build trust in relationships – it will create a safety net for the mistakes you make or the problems that will inevitably come your way.*

✓ *Discipline your children when they are young so they will learn to trust you and their own selves later in life. Always discipline with unconditional love.*

# Strategy 21.

# Maintain an active faith – it is an antidote to failure.

At the end of my first year at the Coast Guard Academy I did something that many of my classmates thought was really dumb. When I told the Chaplain what I had done, he said I had gone too far. But, because of what I did, I had the time of my life that summer in Europe. In looking back on it, what I did solidified my resolve to be free. Given the choice, I would do it again. Unknowingly at that time, I had begun practicing one of the greatest strategies for abundance. Read on to see if you would have done the same as I did.

If you don't believe that failures are meant for your benefit, you will be held captive by mediocrity. It is like having a beautiful sailboat, wonderfully equipped with all of the best rigging and gear, but then not being willing to cast off the lines from their moorings and get underway. If you remain tied to the dock, you will never experience that exhilarating feeling of watching the wind fill the sails as you set a course toward your island paradise.

> *Men are anxious to improve their circumstances, but are unwilling to improve themselves. They therefore remain bound.*
> James Allen

Napoleon Hill conducted research on over 500 successful men and women living in America during the early part of the twentieth century. He was studying them to see what they did in order to bring about their success. He found several definite principles that can be applied to one's life in order to be successful at any endeavor. In his books, *Keys to Success – The 17 Principles of Personal Achievement* and *Think & Grow Rich*, Napoleon Hill indicated that <u>applied faith</u> was "the only known antidote to failure."

Webster defines faith as "a confident belief in the truth, value, or trustworthiness of a person, idea or thing; a belief that does not rest on logical proof or material evidence." The Bible similarly teaches that "faith is the substance of things hoped for, the evidence of things not seen." Both definitions imply that faith is an active expression of a willingness to believe what cannot be scientifically proven. Applied faith therefore starts with a willingness to believe, which is in essence, a decision to believe. Here are three things in which you must apply your faith if you choose to free yourself from mediocrity and to be successful:

1) Believe there is a Creator who designed the universe and all that is in it. He is an unlimited source of knowledge, energy and abundance.
2) Believe in yourself. You are a being who has an unlimited capacity to learn all that you need to know to fulfill your purpose in life.
3) Believe that the whole world was designed to provide abundant life in every respect. The universal laws were established to help you learn from your failures, because each has a seed of opportunity that will bring abundant life.

**Believe there is a Creator.**

Let's analyze each of these so you can see why it is important to have applied faith in all three. We start with *believing there is a Creator*, a God Napoleon Hill called "Infinite Intelligence." The Jewish people call Him "Jehovah Jireh" which means God the Provider. If you do not believe there is a God that is all-knowing, then you will never be able to depend on learning all that you need to know in order to achieve any goal that you might set for yourself. You will be justified in setting limits on your knowledge and will never break free of the mediocrity that was set by your own inaccurate thinking.

On the other hand, if you confidently believe in God, then you will be able to act on your belief by asking for the knowledge and wisdom that you need in order to do what you were meant to do. In the Book of St. James it says, "if anyone lacks wisdom let him ask of God, who gives it freely to all people who ask. But let him ask in faith without doubting ..." You can be assured that God wants to give you wisdom, so you will know what to do with the knowledge that you acquire, and you will use it for your good and the good of others. Believing in God equals unlimited potential for wisdom.

**Believe in yourself.**

Next let's look at *believing in yourself*. If you do not believe in your own self, that you were created for a definite purpose, then you will never begin to reach your potential because you won't even try. There will be a psychological disconnect that will keep you tied to mediocrity.

> *Faith without works is useless ... was not Abraham our father justified by works, when he offered up Isaac his son on the altar? You see that faith was working with his works, and as a result of the works, faith was perfected.*
>
> Saint James

In reality, your true potential for learning is unlimited. The only limit that can be established is the one you impose on yourself. You can learn anything that is needed to fulfill your purpose. You were made in the image of God, and the one and only thing that He gave you complete control over is your mind. If He gave you solitary control over your mind, then you can be certain that He wants you to be in charge of your own mind. Act on your belief in yourself now by deciding to learn whatever it is that you need to know in order to fulfill your purpose in life. Do that and you will set yourself free – you will be SUCCESS BOUND.

**Believe you were meant to have abundant life.**

Last, but not least, you need to *believe you were meant to have abundant life*. If you do not believe that the universe and its laws are meant for your benefit and are unchanging, then you will never be able to improve your life because you won't be able to trust what you learn when you make mistakes. All of nature and the universal laws have been established to help us have abundant life. For instance, you can count on the *Law of Sowing and Reaping* to help you learn and do, learn and do, until you close the gap between the result you expected and the one you got.

I had mentioned in Strategy 8 that the *Law of Tithing* (also known as the *Law of Giving*) was one of the universal laws that you can count on. To illustrate this universal law I will finish the story I started at the beginning of this chapter. The thing that I did at the end of my first year at the Coast Guard Academy, the thing that others thought was dumb, actually proved to me that the *Law of Giving* works.

Prior to departing for the summer on a training cruise to Europe on the Coast Guard's tallship EAGLE, each of us cadets received several hundred dollars to use as spending money at the ports we were going to visit. I had just spent the weekend hosting a group of college students from a school in Maine, who were going to be spending the summer doing missionary work. I felt a strong urge to give them some of the money I had just received since they were giving up their whole summer to serve others and I had the feeling they were going to need the money more than I would. I asked God how much I should give and He told me – ALL OF IT!

> *Generosity during life is very different from generosity in the hour of death; one proceeds from genuine liberality and benevolence, the other from pride or fear.*
> Horace Mann

Even I thought it was a dumb idea at first. Without any money I would be stuck on the ship without any means to go out and have fun or enjoy visiting Europe. Then I had one of those rare moments. I felt as if God were saying, "test Me in this. If you give that money for My work, I promise that you will have the time of your life. Your whole summer will be on Me, you won't need a dime."

How could I refuse an offer like that? I gave all of my money to the missionary team, and as I live today I promise you I had the time of my life. When we sailed into the European ports I was met by people that I had never met before, and I was escorted to fun and exciting places, given meals, taken into homes, driven to Paris and put up for the night. If I hadn't been there myself to witness it, I would be tempted to say unbelievable, but it was true.

What I did gave me the resolve to be free – free of the fear of losing money. I believe that my parents were never able to accumulate much money and were always "just getting by" because they were afraid of poverty. They wanted money, but never had enough. They were bound to mediocrity because they wouldn't give up what little they had to receive more. I wanted to be set free of that fear. I didn't quite know it at the time, but by giving my money away, I was following the *Law of Giving*.

This law says that you must give in order to receive. My friends thought I had gone nuts, that I had become a religious fanatic. Since then, I've practiced the *Law of Giving*, not so it will make me rich, but because it is the right thing to do. I've always had enough money to meet all of my needs and my family's needs. The fear of poverty has been replaced by contentment with what I have and joy in blessing others.

> *I came so that you might have life, and have it more abundantly. I am the good shepherd; the good shepherd lays down His life for His sheep.*
> Jesus Christ

Turn your belief into faith by acting on it. Learn the universal laws and then analyze your life, noting where you have made mistakes or received results different from what you desired. Learn what caused the mistakes, then correct them and try again. By doing this you will continuously improve and are guaranteed to be a success in whatever you set out to do. Start out by analyzing the purpose of your life and reducing the gap between what you are doing now and what you are meant to do.

The more you act on your faith in an all-knowing God, the more you will open up to receive wisdom. The more wisdom you acquire, the more self-confidence you will have and the more you will act on your purpose. The more you act on your purpose in life, the more power you will receive to achieve more. The more you achieve, the more courage you will find to step into the unknown, where you are bound to make mistakes. By making mistakes you will turn to the all-knowing God for wisdom. It is a wonderful spiral that leads you to abundant life.

There is another wonderful cycle. It says in the Bible that the truth will set you free. As Americans, we live in a society that celebrates truth. One of those truths, as proclaimed in the *Declaration of Independence,* is the pursuit of happiness. In fact, we call it an *inalienable right*, which is something that can't be taken from us. Pursuit is indicative of action. Thus, by taking action in what you believe (applied faith) you will acquire happiness, satisfaction and peace of mind, which bring about a success consciousness. Being success conscious will give you more freedom to continue the pursuit of happiness, which is acting on your faith. Acting on your faith will increase your capacity for faith and the cycle toward an abundant life will continue.

Faith is not something that can be created by you. The Bible says that God gives us the "gift of faith." Since it is a gift, it must be appropriated. I believe you appropriate faith by preparing your mind to receive it. After receiving the gift you open it up and use it. You would probably feel bad if you gave someone a gift and they left it unopened. Once received, faith is meant to be used. When you use your gift of faith you make God very happy. You will have life, and have it more abundantly as the Bible promises.

**Practice positive affirmations.**

How do we mentally prepare to receive faith? I have discovered that one of the ways to appropriate faith is to practice positive affirmations in my life. I learned some time ago to use positive affirmations when I talk to myself so that I will be prepared to believe. Specially devised affirmations have helped me to improve my thinking, and therefore, the world around me. One of my favorite affirmations goes like this: "I know how to recognize an opportunity and I have the ambition to explore its possibilities and to learn all that I need to know in order to turn the opportunity into ABUNDANT LIFE for myself, my family, and my friends."

That affirmation has changed my life and has brought me and my family success and abundant life in many ways. It has prepared my mind and heart to receive faith and then act on it. I believe that affirmations have helped me feel a strong confidence that each failure, problem, struggle, etc. has a purpose. That purpose, as you now know, was to bring a gift – a little seed of opportunity to nurture faith into a life-giving benefit.

If you practice positive affirmations, you can make living outside of mediocrity a habit for yourself. Consider developing your own affirmations, which incorporate managing failures so that they become seeds of opportunities that you can grow into abundant life for you and your loved ones. You can learn more about how to use positive affirmations from Brian Tracy's book, *Maximum Achievement*.

> *The faith in which we can live bravely and die in peace must be a certainty, so far as it professes to be a faith at all, or it is nothing*
> Froude

You cannot explain God, but by faith you can believe that He exists. You cannot explain your ability to do something that you have never done before, but by faith you can believe you will accomplish your major purpose in life. When you accept the existence of faith even though you can't explain it, you will receive its benefits. As you increase your capacity for faith you will experience a sense of contentment and well-being that can only come from a higher power than yourself.

In the Book of Proverbs it says, "A righteous man falls seven times, and rises again." I believe that part of the reason people of faith get back on their feet and try again is because of discipline and persistence. But I also believe that when your faith increases, the failures that might otherwise cause you to trip and fall become "touch stones" of success, rather than stumbling blocks.

As we learned earlier, faith is believing with your mind and then acting with your body. And like your body and mind, your faith becomes stronger as you exercise it. Begin with little "acts of faith" and you will be less apprehensive. Believe in the goodness of God, in other people, and in yourself. Eventually, as you learn to trust your ability to apply your faith, you will achieve what you desire and abundant life and love will be yours.

✓ *Have faith in an all-knowing God, in yourself, and in the world in which you live.*

✓ *Without applied faith you will not be able to launch toward success. The way you exercise your faith is by using it. Start out with little steps of faith and keep stretching your comfort zone.*

✓ *Use positive affirmations to prepare your mind to receive faith. In the same way that you never outgrow the need for healthy food, you should never outgrow the need for feeding your mind good and healthy things that help your faith to grow.*

# Biblical Bonus

## Admit Spiritual Failure and Your Eternal Success Is Assured.

Although I have made Biblical references throughout this book, I am concluding with an extra strategy that relates our ultimate and everlasting success directly to the Bible. If you are certain of your eternal success, then you can skip this and go right to the AFTERWARD. However, if you are not certain of what will happen to you when you die, then please read what I have to say with an open mind and heart. Remember the words Jesus spoke to believers, "In my Father's house are many mansions, if it were not so I would have told you, for I go to prepare a place for you." I want to make sure one of those mansions has been reserved for you.

There is a saying in the Bible that goes like this, "What does it profit a man, if he gains the whole world and yet loses his soul?" When Jesus was teaching He warned, "Beware of every form of greed, for not even when a person has abundance does his life consist of his possessions."

> *My objective in life is not to have a spiritual life that is separate from the rest of my life.*
> Ed McCracken

Abundant life is having it all, not just a lot of money, big house, nice car, and other worldly riches. In the Bible there is a story about a rich man who came to see Jesus and asked Him, "What good thing must I do to have eternal life?" Jesus told him that he had to do the things that the Scripture instructed. The rich man replied that he had done what he had been told all of his life about keeping God's Commandments. Then Jesus told him that if he wanted to be certain of eternal life, he needed to sell all of his possessions and give them to the poor and then be His disciple. Unfortunately it says that the rich man went away saddened because he had great wealth. The Bible doesn't mention anything more about that person, but Jesus told the people who were listening that it is more difficult for a rich man to get into heaven than for a camel to pass through the eye of a needle.

Many Christians have interpreted that story to mean that money is evil and that they should not want it. I believe this is not a reasonable understanding. From the rest of the Bible we understand that money itself is neutral, it is neither good nor bad. Money takes on the character of the person who uses it. It is how money is spent that makes it either good or bad. I believe that Jesus was trying to get the rich man to see that when it comes to eternal security, he must not depend on anything in this world, because nothing of this world can buy eternal life and nothing can go with him when he dies.

Jesus was trying to teach the rich man (and us) the *Law of Abundance*, which means that the Creator has provided everything we need. The more we realize that God is the ultimate provider of everything, the more we can "let go and let God." For some people it is a very difficult concept to understand that the more they let God provide for them the more they have.

For example, children share in the wealth of their parents. All through their lives they only need to ask, and it is provided for them. Parents are happy to provide good things for their children. I always had food enough and a comfortable home. When I became a teenager I asked for and received a car to drive when I needed one. I didn't own the car, but as long as I acted responsibly, I was able to use it as if I owned it. Slowly I learned how to become responsible for myself, but while I was a part of my parent's household, I had privileges that I didn't have when I became independent. When children become independent they give up the right to ask and they have to work for everything they need. I never could have afforded the car or even a small portion of what was provided if I had to do it on my own as I grew up. If we remain independent from God, we must struggle for everything we own. And, in the end we have to give it all up, because nothing can go with us when we die.

> *When in need of wisdom call God's toll free number – Jeremiah 33:3, "Call to Me, and I will answer you, and I will tell you great and mighty things, which you do not know.*
>
> Unknown

God wants to be your Heavenly Father and to provide for you. In order for this to happen, you need to become a part of His family. Jesus said that unless you become as children, you cannot enter the kingdom of God. When a religious leader inquired about this, Jesus told him that he had to be born into the physical world and also born again into the spiritual world. I had it explained to me this way, "If you are born twice, you will die once; but if you are born only once, then you will die twice – both physically and spiritually."

A person can not DO anything, BE anybody, or HAVE anything that will ever be good enough to force his or her way into God's eternal kingdom. You have to become a member of His family, His way. In the Gospel of St. Matthew it is recorded that Jesus said, "not every one who says to Me, 'Lord, Lord,' will enter the kingdom of heaven; only those who do the will of My Father who is in heaven [will enter]." By believing in Jesus and doing God's will, you become a part of God's family; then you have all of the rights and privileges of being God's child. It is like being royalty; nothing is held back that you desire. Jesus said, "Anything you ask for in My name, you will receive."

Similarly, when a person becomes a member of the military, he is given privileges that go along with his responsibilities. In the naval services, when given command of a ship or aircraft, an officer is able to do with that ship or aircraft whatever is desired within the limits of responsibility. Some privileges can be far more valuable than one could ever afford on one's own. For example, the Admiral who is in charge of the Coast Guard units in Hawaii is given an absolutely gorgeous home next to the Diamond Head Lighthouse, overlooking Waikiki bay. He is the envy of even the rich people on the Island of Oahu. He uses that home as if he owns it, but even on an Admiral's salary, he could not come close to buying a home like that. Similarly God can provide "riches" far greater than we could ever earn on our own.

Jesus wants to be our "Commander in Chief" and wants to give us all of the privileges that go along with the responsibilities we are given. It takes faith to become His follower. In the Bible, a story is told about a soldier (Roman Centurion) who went to Jesus to ask Him to heal his sick servant. Jesus offered to go to the soldier's home to heal his servant, but the soldier felt that it was inappropriate (since he was not a Jew). He then suggested that Jesus just say the words, like a commander giving orders to his soldiers, and it would be done. Jesus told the soldier, and those standing by, that He had not seen such faith in all of Israel. Jesus immediately spoke the words and the soldier's servant was healed, though He was a long distance from the servant.

You can prepare your mind to acquire the faith needed to believe, just like that soldier did. It is not difficult. It starts with a desire to believe. Decide that you want to be eternally secure and to live forever, just like Jesus said was possible in the Bible. You don't need to be physically present with Him to experience His power. Even though He spoke the words written in the Bible a long time ago, they are still just as relevant and meaningful today.

> *If God is for us, who could be against us? He who did not spare His own Son, but delivered Him up for us all, how will He not freely give us all things through Him?*
>
> Romans 8:31, 32

For those not familiar with the Bible, let me point out some important concepts that will help you to prepare your mind to acquire the faith to believe in God's eternal salvation. In the Book of Romans it says, "All have sinned and fall short of the glory of God." When Adam and Eve disobeyed God and ate from the tree that gave them (and their descendants) the knowledge of good and evil, we all became sinners. Man became aware of how to do evil, which lost us our birthright to God's eternal kingdom. God wants to restore our birthright to us. But we need to be changed. God has made a way to change us.

In the Book of Isaiah, God said, "Come let us reason together, although your sins are red like scarlet, they will be made as white as snow." God had given man time and opportunity to be good on his own, but it didn't work. Even sacrificing animals and other things we cared about could not make us good enough. It was just a temporary solution that dealt with the symptoms, not the root cause of the problem. Another way had to be developed. That is where the Christmas story fits in, of Jesus leaving heaven and being born into the world. In the Gospel (the Good News) according to St. John, he writes, "For God so loved the world that He sent His only son so that all who believe in Him might not perish, but have everlasting life."

Jesus Christ is God and man at the same time. Although He was born as naturally as you or I, His Father is God Himself. That gave Jesus the ability to know right from wrong, even as a young child. Jesus lived a sinless life. He was the only person ever to live that was able to "be good" on His own. He also had an extraordinary faith, because He believed with His mind and followed through with action.

Jesus became a threat to the religious leaders of His time, because they were trying to control God through their own rules. They convinced the Roman Governor to sentence Jesus to death on a cross. Since Jesus was completely innocent, His death became the perfect sacrifice, which was able to remove the sins of any person who believes that Jesus died on their behalf. To prove that Jesus was God and not just another martyr, God publicly raised Him from the dead, showing the world that He had conquered sin and death for everyone who believes.

In the Book of First John, the author tells us "…the blood of Jesus, God's Son cleanses us from all sin. If we say that we have no sin then we are lying to ourselves and the truth is not in us. But, if we confess our sins, then Jesus is faithful and righteous and able to forgive us our sins and to cleanse us from all unrighteousness." Jesus told His disciples "I am the way, the truth, and the life, no man comes to the Father, but by Me." That is, believing in Jesus Christ and recognizing His death on the cross on our behalf, is our only means of freeing ourselves from sinfulness – from our eternal failures.

> ... the Spirit also helps our weakness; for we do not know how to pray as we should, but the Spirit Himself intercedes for us with groanings too deep for words; and He who searches the hearts knows what the mind of the Spirit is, because He intercedes for the saints according to the will of God.
> Romans 8:26, 27

God is "all-knowing" and is therefore the ultimate source of all wisdom. When we believe that Jesus suffered and died for our failures, God the Holy Spirit is sent to become a part of our inner being as part of the free gift of God's salvation through Christ. Jesus said, in the Gospel of St. John, that the Holy Spirit would be sent to be our Teacher and our Helper to give us the power to turn from our failures and sins. It also is told in the Book of Acts, when the first disciples received the Holy Spirit, they received divine power to boldly act out their faith. By communicating directly with God the Holy Spirit, we attain the wisdom we need to live the abundant life Jesus came to bring to us.

Believing that Jesus lived in Israel and then died on a cross just outside the walls of Jerusalem about 2000 years ago is one thing, but now you need to act on that belief. Faith is both believing and acting on your belief. Unfortunately, acting on one's belief in God is not as simple as it might sound; at least it wasn't for me.

When I was an Eighth Grader in Hawaii, a Japanese boy told me about Jesus in a similar way as above, but it didn't make sense at first. I was convinced at the time that science had all of the answers. However, the more I learned about science, the more I came to understand that there has to be a master Creator.

Even Darwin's new theory of evolution only made sense if there was a pattern in nature that everything evolved into, which required a Creator of that pattern. The possibility of things happening in nature by themselves, as Darwin proposed, was a mathematical impossibility; there was too much randomness. In fact, I discovered that it took more faith to believe there isn't a Creator – that all of the universe is a random mix of time and chance – than to believe that there is one. I came to realize the truth about myself. I didn't want to believe in God, because that meant that I would have to give up my attempt to be one, which is the condition that all of us are born into. We all have that sinful mentality.

After several years of learning about various religions, I finally turned to Christ, because Jesus was the only man who proved Himself to be God and guaranteed salvation. All other religions just talked about life after death, but they provided no proofs and no guarantees. I wanted to be certain of what I believed. I read in the Book of Romans, "... if you confess with your mouth Jesus as Lord, and believe in your heart that God raised Him from the dead, you shall be saved."

> ... if you are living according to the flesh, you must die; but if by the Spirit you are putting to death the deeds of the body, you will live. For all who are being led by the Spirit of God, these are the Sons of God.
>
> Romans 7:13, 14

When I decided to act on my belief and become a part of God's family, I prayed a simple prayer that went something like this, "Dear God, I know that I am a sinner and I can't be righteous on my own. I now believe that you sent Jesus into the world to die for my sins. I ask for forgiveness and believe that you will wash me clean and help me to live a life that is worthy of being in your family."

I was later baptized in a church that I attended regularly, studied the Bible with other believers, and started acting out my faith daily by praying and serving God as best I knew how. I know that I still have a sin nature and still make mistakes, but I also know that I am SUCCESS BOUND for all eternity. You can be too. I invite you to act on your belief in God today and become a disciple of Jesus Christ.

✓ *Become a part of God's family and do not claim ownership to anything, just stewardship. You will give up ownership of earthly possessions, but you will gain riches in the kingdom of God beyond your wildest dreams, both here on earth and in the world to come.*

✓ *To have guaranteed eternal success, believe in Jesus and become His disciple. It will give you the ability to think clearly and to have active faith, a main ingredient to success and an abundant life.*

# AFTERWORD

Dear Reader of SUCCESS BOUND,

I am so glad you read this book. Even if you are not able to remember all of the strategies and put them to work right away, you will have them available to you when the need arises. I recommend you review them every so often to refresh your memory.

I believe that one of my seeds of opportunity is this book. I have been nurturing it along by faith and hope so it will be a benefit to you – my friend. It is my greatest wish that you will receive this book and put its lessons into practice so you too will know the success and abundant life that managing failures <u>can</u> <u>and</u> <u>will</u> bring.

I hope that through this book you might have found the motivation to discover your major purpose in life. I speak from experience when I say, "Sincerity of purpose can make you immune to the fear of failure." As you take on a proactive attitude and exercise control over your failures, you to will discover that you are SUCCESS BOUND – there will be no stopping you – nothing is impossible for you.

If you felt these strategies were valuable to you, please pass them on to <u>your</u> friends. Teaching these truths will help you to learn them better and it will indicate that you have made a commitment to following them.

Also, please check out my website http://www.RandyGilbert.com for lots of other valuable information and check back from time to time at http://www.Success-Bound.com to get updates to this book.

If you have had a special experience about how a failure in your life was turned into an opportunity for success and you want to share it with others, please send me an email.

Address it to:

Randy@DrProactive.com.

Perhaps one of your failures taught you another aspect about managing failures that you would like to share with others in a revised edition of this book. If so, I would be glad to consider including your experience and providing appropriate credit.

I am also the editor of a free electronic magazine (ezine) called Proactive Success. Hopefully you've been able to see from this book the importance of proactive thinking in helping you to achieve success and abundance. If you want to become a better proactive thinker then please subscribe by sending an email to:

proactivesuccess@postermaster-email.com

Thank you, and God bless you every day as you receive joy and abundance while achieving your success.

May Success and Abundance Be Your Destiny,

*Randy Gilbert*
*http://www.RandyGilbert.com*